HIDDEN PATH

A personal spiritual journey

By

Vanessa Graham

OSHADHI PUBLISHING

First published in United Kingdom in 2007

Published by **Oshadhi Publishing**
Oshadhi Meditation Centre, Saddlers Meadow,
West End Lane, Henfield, West Sussex BN5 9RE

Website see www.energyenhancement.co.uk

ISBN

978-0-9555617-0-2

Foreword

The reason for writing this book is that I wanted to touch people's hearts. Although this book is about my own personal spiritual journey, I hope that you the reader can relate to many of the everyday happenings and find a resonance of them in your life.

We share and suffer similar life events, sometimes feeling isolated and disconnected and I wanted to show through my experience of them, that I have developed a greater spiritual understanding of myself and my life. Our spirit was given our physical body so that our spirit could experience life and living to its fullest. It has been a quite journey to come to this understanding and I hope that you will share this with me, using this book to reflect on your own life experiences and to allow your spiritual side to be discovered.

Living with Uncertainty

How to start to write a book about my journey into meditation and beyond? Who would be interested? I thought perhaps I could create an alter ego who would illustrate my journey and make it into a quest, that would be more exciting and interesting but that would not be the truth. It has to be told just how it is, so that the reader will know it's true and has actually happened. Why would I want to write down my journey? Because it is a secret journey that very few people know about. I live with family and friends and they know I do yoga, meditate and go on retreats but very rarely am I questioned about what I do. So it is for those that I write this down, that my invisible life journey is made visible, that others may come to understand it. By charting my spiritual journey I would like to encourage others on the same path. That the reader can share the experiences in the light of their own lives and for spiritual recognition to occur.

We are born a spiritual being yet in today's busy world we somehow seem to lose that connection but it is always there awaiting for us to find it. Spirituality is not separate from life, it is life and we have come into existence at this time to develop our own spirituality. I can say those words in hindsight as I have come to a realisation of this. Through meditation I have been able to review my life in this light, this book will be a witness to that process. I have been able to understand the events in my life, have been for a reason and it was up to me to learn the lesson they were trying to teach me. You grow in spirituality (Consciousness) by experiencing difficult situations and learning from them. Experience and wisdom come at a cost of experiencing pain. But it can be viewed as a growing pains, something you have to go through in order to grow spiritually.

In writing the recent sequence of events down, I will be able to understand more fully their significance and bearing on my life. It has been a learning experience way outside the scope of my normal existence. For a long time I separated my 'normal' life from my spiritual life – I kept them apart, I even formed a whole new group of friends and acquaintances with whom I could relate to spiritually. It was with these like minded people I could discuss the ancient scriptures and spiritual matters as easily as I could discuss what I had just bought in the supermarket or what I watched on TV the previous night, as I did with my other friends.

This fragmentation of my life came to a head, I had to stand up and declare that a spiritual path was the most important thing in my life. I was dedicating my life to it. Needless to say those around me thought it was the menopause, depression or a breakdown or all three. In fact I had just had enough of being two people at once. I have been a mother and wife, been part of an extended family and have many close and long standing friendships. I hope they will be the first to read this book and then they will have a greater understanding of what spirituality means to me.

Using the word spiritual means realising you are more than the mind and body. There is a presence that exists in every one of us, which is part of a universal presence, I shall call it consciousness (although it has many other names). There is no separation between our physical body and our spirit. A spiritual journey involves understanding you are part of the spiritual essence that pervades everything. It is a continual learning process whereby an open mind is the best mind to have. Throwing out all past ideas, beliefs, and preconceptions to leave space for the new to enter. This is where meditation helps, by clearing your mind and creating space, presence can reveal itself to you.

A misguided idea of meditation is to sit cross-legged and let your mind go blank. Anyone who has tried it can vouch that your legs get painful and your mind remains full of thoughts. It does not happen over night, it takes practice and diligence, then one day you enter a peaceful space for a few seconds which make you think 'wow that was nice, I would like that again' and that experience can maintain your practice. When it was suggested I should teach meditation, I had this concept that I must know all the answers first. I don't, but I can be good enough. I would not set myself up to be an expert when I would be only a few steps ahead of those I teach for meditation. When I teach I stress meditation is more than just techniques for quietening the mind and body, it is a way of life and this book will show how it has been for me.

When I decided to write the book I wanted it to be an organic process. I did not just want to write it down, I wanted to show how my life unfolds and continues to unfold, even as I actually write. Emails, books, conversations can all act as triggers to write and I wanted to include these. It can be the unexpected that reveals so much. Chance encounters can influence ones life, they can be signposts that point the way. I was listening to a swami speak and he told a story of the wind blowing a newspaper towards his legs and it became stuck to his ankles, no matter how much he tried to shake it off it would not budge. Eventually he bent down to pick it off, his eyes were caught by a short paragraph of words and those very words were the ones he needed to hear. They made a great impact on his life and they were the focus of his talk to us that day, saying be open to the messages that are sent daily to you to help you on your spiritual path but you have to be able to see them when they arrive and listen to what is being said.

I am always amazed at the unusual route these messages take to get to me and I have included some of them as I write. Life evolves, it is not set in stone, it is being open to the unexpected and to be ready to learn from life's messengers. Be it a book falling into ones hand, a piece of paper turning up out of the blue, tripping over a stone or any silly thing that happens which can get easily overlooked. Sometimes I silently ask for help and it's as if by a miracle it occurs, I am not talking about big things like health but smaller things. I asked for triggers to enable me to actually start writing and lo and behold they are falling like raindrops from the sky. Not a downpour more of a steady drip.

Through meditation and yoga I have started to get the feeling that I am working with the universe whereas previously I always thought it was working against me. This feeling has developed into more, as if the universe is expressing itself through me, I am part and parcel of the whole scene not just a separate entity. All the ancient Vedic teachings point to wholeness and unity. An existence of non duality which has provided my background knowledge just as they have done to those before me for thousands of years.

In this book I want to show that meditation is a living, breathing practice. It is organic and evolves with time, often when you are least expecting it. It is life changing in ways that you would never have expected. My life has totally opened up, I meet and mix with people and swamis I would never imagined previously. I have travelled to Greece, Spain and Argentina to increase my experience and knowledge. It has given me the courage to be more creative in art and writing. I am no longer ruled by the limited ego, I have changed to allow life's energies to be expressed through me. I no longer want to be in charge of my life, I am happier to go with the flow and see where it takes me. But there is an underlying current in my life a quest for personal growth and reaching my own potential. I want to find out the reason for my existence, I do not want to just sit back and let my life pass me by. I want to develop spiritually, to gain first hand experience and knowledge. I am open to change and the unknown. This book is the journey of where I have travelled so far.

Table of Contents

Chapter 1

Fly on the windowpane

Lost in thought wondering how to start to write my book, I watched a fly trying to get out of the closed window, it perpetually kept hitting itself against the window glass. It flew away then soon returned trying to force its way out. As I watched I came to see myself as that fly continually hitting myself on the glass also trying to get away. I flew in through the open door but seemed determined to find another route out other than where I entered.

Originally I saw the windowpane as an analogy of the consciousness (a deep meditative state) I wanted to enter through meditation. I always knew it was there but it was invisible, I would try many different methods in order to enter it but the problem came in the trying. You cannot enter consciousness just by trying; you can only make yourself available to it and hope or believe it will ultimately happen. Continual faith is needed that it will ultimately occur, faith is needed to sustain on the long journey to spiritual awakening.

There is no magic wand that is going to be waved one day and that enlightenment will happen just like that. It is a lifetime's journey where you continually learn ways to make yourself available to it. Do not expect this journey to be easy. It can be challenging and enlivening but never easy. I have had to turn myself inside out to discover who I really am and it is an ongoing process. I have had to revisit, and relive past experiences to find out what made me the way I was, in order to bring about change. With that realisation I had the choice to stay or change the way I was.

The reason why I see consciousness as a transparent windowpane is that there have been occasions when in meditation or a deep sleep state, I have felt I have come into contact with it. The feeling is that I am always on the outside of it, separated it by a glass wall. Everything is so bright and vibrant on the other side, I can sense I am close to something way outside of my experience of unimaginable beauty but can only look on. It is experiences like this that help to continue my practice. They are not something easily expressed by words and one is hesitant to do so, as by making them material they lose their essence.

Change is easier said than done, it takes innumerable tries and many failures. If you want change to happen you have to want it badly enough and then it will happen. You overcome the failed attempts and try again, slowly the wanted change will happen and by practicing that change, it becomes part of your life. My journey of self-realisation has been just that. In my life many of the small changes have added up to the big change and that's why I decided to write a book to show how I have achieved this.

I did not want to make this book a guide to self-realization, as everyone's own journey is personal to them. This book is about my personal journey and the changes that have happened in my life. I have tried not to use formal academic words that are associated with the processes that happened, as they are just labels. Words can be empty ink marks upon a page unless you relate to them, a word is only a signpost to take you to what is beyond them. I have tried not to get hooked on key words like enlightenment, as how could a mere word encompass all that it contains? It is so vast and mainly uncharted territory for the writer of it, my only advice would be always to look beyond the word. Peep over the garden wall of the word and see for yourself the proliferation of sights, smells, sounds that exist, experience it for yourself. Believe no-one else's description of it, find out what it means for you. I love words and could play around with them for ages, just trying to find the right one that captures what I wanted to say. Words can dance; bring about emotions, stir feelings as words have past associations but you need to rub the sleep from your eyes, open them wide and look with new insight.

So I am this fly bruising my wings, as I hit the windowpane of consciousness but do I give up? It is unlikely that the easy route will be given, that the window will be opened and I will become enlightened. Eventually I turned around and looked for another route out, or perversely in. The journey of self-realization has similar aspects to the fly. You always hope that someone else will do all the hard work of the journey for you but there is no cop out clause, you have to do it for yourself. You come to understand there is a simpler way other than making irritating buzzing noises in the hope that some one will let you out. Turn around and go out the door you came in from.

The start of the journey to self-realization is learning to turn round, turn inwards instead of the perpetual turning outwards. As human beings we continually seek satisfaction from outside objects, sensations, situations or people. We hope that from these we will be able to feel complete that they'll fill that empty hole that we feel within our being.

That empty hollow feeling that lies within each person is our soul calling. It's a calling to be connected with who you really are but first of all you have to find out who you really are. You are mind, body and soul but the soul part of you connects you to a consciousness that encompasses all the individual souls together, they are one and part of it all. There is no separation between the individual soul and consciousness, only unity exists. Through meditation you come in touch with that unity. By experiencing it for yourself, you will know that it is so. It is of no use being told it exists by someone else, you need to experience it for yourself, to feel its presence.

There is a choice to form this connection for yourself. You might want to link it to religion and praying but when you pray it involves the 'mind activity' of words. The connection I am trying to describe happens in the silence and stillness beyond the words. You need to put yourself in the silence and stillness through meditation to be available to the consciousness that exists. When that connection is formed, life takes on a deeper depth and meaning. Everyday life can be carried out but it is enriched, smaller occurrences that can be appreciated with gratitude. The soul's emptiness is no longer felt when it is united with the consciousness that exists, life can be lived to its fullest.

When approaching middle age, and with my children moving on to new stages in their lives, I felt the emptiness of my soul more keenly. I had always felt there was more to life than just existence. There were the pleasures in life but equally there were the pains. In youth you are less aware of the painful side of life, I was optimistic and found living enjoyable. With children and a mortgage, life took on a different perspective. I was fortunate not to have to work for a living and was able to devote myself to bringing up my two children. With family life being my focus, I could only hear the faint callings of my soul and these were often dismissed. As I grew older and came to experience suffering and death of others personally, the question rose 'what is life really about?' Life is full of problems, large and small; each family can provide their own evidence of these. When I looked around I saw no one was immune to problems and suffering, at whatever level. The next question ultimately arose 'why were there problems?'

Pain and pleasure are two sides of the same coin. Only by having pain can pleasure be appreciated, each are needed to highlight the other. Meditation can help you see the coin not its two separate faces, it is a distancing yourself from the pleasure/pain cycle but that is another story. A different explanation given to me as to why family life had to be so problematic was that it was given to us as the quickest way to enlightenment. I can vouch, to it's validity, as over the years I have learnt to deal with life's problems by turning inwards, where help is at hand. The spiritual essence never leaves us and is always there to be drawn on in difficult times.

When I started learning about meditation I took my major problems to my guru and asked how I could deal with them through meditation and he gave me guidance how I could. They were problems linked to my father's suffering with cancer and his ultimate death, also my son's depression; how I could cope and how I could help them. Life around this time consisted of many family deaths and my watching their suffering. It seems that at a certain time in your life the older level in one's family dies away and you yourself become that older level. I wondered where that time had gone and how I had come to this point in such a short while. In my early fifties, relations and friends were dying suddenly and others had major illnesses. Life became precious not to be taken for granted, as who knew what the future would hold. There arose vulnerability about my age, nothing was guaranteed, I might not live until my eighties and even if I did many health problems could arise. The bravado of youth had completely disappeared, at times my future looked bleak but meditation had helped me deal with this negativity, to appreciate the many gifts life has to give.

Family life is full of problems, particularly involving relationship dynamics. I learnt to drop my expectation of being a perfect housewife and mother accepting that I was good enough under the circumstances. Even if I were perfect my children would have still been able to find fault with me. Maybe they will hold my short temper against me or perhaps the fun birthday parties might outweigh it, who knows. Through meditation I have been able to let go of the past, as it is now in the past. It is the present that is important and I have come to value the relationships that I have, in the here and now.

In following a spiritual life I've had to renegotiate the relationships I have had with my close family members. It has been an internal process most of the time and I often feel alone in doing it, as it is not visible to those close to me. Often I am dismissed as a bit weird with worries I might join a dubious religious sect. There seemed no desire from them to learn more about what I am doing. But I am not looking for converts or to win praise, I just go on making the minor adjustments within myself that will enhance our relationships together. Meditation has helped me let go of interfering or trying to control their lives. I would not say I always get it right, only that I am aware when I might be interfering or controlling and try to avoid it. That's the thing with problems, you solve one and you get another.

I used to view problems in a very negative light, 'oh no not another one, why me?' kind of way. When I was told family problems are the quickest way to enlightenment, I thought someone had lost the plot there. How wrong I was. Problems are the coalface of our daily life. Big or small they can be tackled by turning inwards and meditating. Not by meditating on the problem itself but by dropping into silence and stillness, which allows a resolution of the problem to surface. In this quiet space a strength is gained to deal with larger problems. Sometimes, even as if by magic they can be resolved.

When my father was dying, I went with him by ambulance to a London hospital for radiography treatment. It was not something I was looking forward to; he was in a lot of discomfort and had to wait in a corridor on a hard trolley for hours. Just when you think it can't get any worse, the ambulance could not collect us and we had to wait in a small room. My father was in great pain by then and needed morphine. I was at a total loss what to do, when in walked a Sister who I had never seen before, to ask if she could do anything. I was so grateful to see her and she sorted the morphine out. Her presence seemed like a much needed miracle. We had another three hours to wait. When my father was fast asleep, I opened a spiritual book that I'd been advised to read for such a situation. It was a book that I had difficulty understanding but somehow those hours disappeared in an instant. I was deeply grateful that I was able to come through a difficult situation and be there for my father throughout. Now that he's gone I can feel his presence, in the silence and stillness that exists. Our love for each other will never die.

Our relationship had its highs and lows but our love carried us through our difficulties. Hopefully that can be said for most family relationships, love unites and holds a family together. When young people set out on their own in life there seems a need to find a partner to weather life's problems. It can be explained away in biological or emotional terms. Everyone wants to be loved, they set out to find a partner who will love them and who in turn they can love. As the saying goes 'Love makes the world go round', yet many remain oblivious to the universal love that is available through consciousness.

I started to get an inkling of it through meditation, but it was only when I was at a very low point that I was first on the receiving end of it. I had a very stressful year with the marriage of my daughter and various relationship problems. The day after the last wedding guest left I crumbled, I just had to get away from everything and everyone so I took myself off in a caravan alone. I was in quite a bad state and did not care where I stopped, ending up an isolated, dubious spot. I just wanted to be alone and had no hope of sleeping. Yet when I laid down the first night I became aware that I was loved, not by any person but by something much greater. It was a feeling of being loved that was attached to no one. It was all encompassing, I felt really cared for and despite my situation, I felt accompanied. That same feeling continued, particularly coming to the fore when I most needed it at night. It makes my heart stir when I remember it.

So there are two kinds of love, the personal and the universal. The universal love is continual, ever flowing – it does not fluctuate with the vagaries of human nature and it is there for everyone; it's only a matter of connecting with it. Nature abounds with love and that's why its beauty – the setting sun, the luminous full moon, autumn trees, refreshes us; the list is endless.

Human love can cause conflict whilst universal love is serene. Being in touch with universal love makes one less dependant on receiving human love, it alleviates loneliness. It does not have to be linked through a God, it can be felt directly. I was on the underground recently when a young religious man entered to exclaim God loved everyone. It was a Sunday and his eyes contained a glazed stare of a strong religious belief. He continued that Jesus was the mediator of God's love. Through meditation you do not need a mediator; you can experience it for yourself directly.

Love can make us feel secure, being unloved leads to feelings of insecurity and no one wants to feel insecure. Human feelings can be fragmentary or transitory which cause pain, even in permanent relationships, partners cause each other pain. Universal love contrasts as it is consistent and pain free. Pain cannot be avoided in whatever form it takes, but the constancy of universal love helps when dealing with life's problems. We can be secure in that knowledge of being loved universally, we just do not know it until you have connected directly with it. It is there all the time for everyone.

Life's problems abound. There is no escape from them and one thing is for sure they do not go away unless they are resolved. This is an area where I have found meditation most useful. It has helped me deal with many minor problems in a calmer manner but its real help lies in tackling the major problems that life throws at us. In fact perversely the bigger problems you get the better your meditation works for you. In desperation I turned inwards to deal with difficult problems and the reason I did turn inwards was because there was nowhere else to turn. In the stillness and silence, the problems can work towards its resolution without all the 'mind chatter' that goes on; without all the tied up emotions and feelings that are attached to the problem. The more difficult a problem creates a greater need to turn inwards through meditation.

Initially, I perpetuated my old habit of turning over the problem in my mind, worrying, fretting, and thinking about it all the time especially during the night. In fact just getting myself into a state on top of the problem itself. On getting to the end of my tether and realising this process was not working, I tried turning inwards. It seems silly although I was told meditation would help resolve problems, I would not believe it and kept replaying my old ways of doing things. Only by getting desperate enough did I try an alternative method. Once I realised meditation did actually help, there was no turning back. I could then understand the relevance that problems can pave the way to enlightenment, that more problems give rise to quicker progress. It gives you the momentum and reason to sustain your practice, as well as gaining the benefits.

So you see I was that fly perpetually banging my head against my old habitual behaviour that I had always used, it did not matter that it did not work. I had the belief that if I tried hard enough things would improve but they did not. Meditation taught me to step back from what I was doing, to see it in a new light and to question was it really in my best interests to do the same that I had always done. To actually realise there was an alternative way to dealing with life's problems and with this realisation, I had taken the first step on my spiritual journey.

Chapter 2

Knowing

Let knowing be your guide. Deep inside me I always knew that there was a deeper depth to living than just existing. I knew but did not know then what I knew. Knowing is consciousness's way of directly communicating to you. Although it is sometimes heard as words in your head and seems to be listened by your ears, it is much more than that. It is more of your whole being acknowledging something already exists spiritually within you, you know. I always knew that when I reached fifty my life would dramatically change. Throughout all the years I never doubted it but it was something that I put to the back of my mind. I questioned at times was it wishful thinking, that some bolt out of the blue would strike me and everything would change but I just waited to see if it would happen.

I was a wife and mother happily fulfilling all my roles but always there was the feeling that there is more to life than this. What more? I could not imagine, but somehow I tied it in with reaching fifty that by then I would know. I had always imagined that enlightenment would suddenly come if you were a chosen one, it would be something that was given to you by the powers that be. I never bothered to conceive what enlightenment might consist of it was just a handy label to use on a blissful state that I thought to exist. Anyway it was for special unique people not for a housewife and mother living an ordinary life in a rural village in England.

As I approached fifty my life was gradually beginning to change, my two children had grown up and were independent. No more school runs or ferrying them from place to place gave me extra freedom. My yoga practice was established, I had been introduced to various spiritual teachers and through their books my knowledge was widening. It was not something I directly chose; it just evolved, It was something I was drawn to. I never set out to become spiritual, but I now had space in my life, I realised that the spiritual element of existence was being ignored by me. As I read spiritual books I felt nourished by them. Often I did not understand the concepts they were using and I struggled to get my brain round what they had to say. If I left that aside, there was something beyond the words that was communicating itself to me.

It came back to 'the knowing'; that what was being conveyed was something big and important, life changing in fact. Through experience I can trust 'the knowing' that exists, that its communications are pure and in my best interests. It is not voices in my head or aliens trying to speak to me from outer space; silly notions have to be put aside and to be open to what actually is. Knowing is found deep within silence and stillness, meditative awareness opens a direct path of communication to it but do not expect it to be like a telephone conversation. When the need arises I offer an important issue to its presence and wait and see what reveals itself to me. It is not instantaneous, an answer might take years to reveal itself but I feel I have been heard.

Patience is always needed. At today's fast pace when we often expect everything by yesterday it is often difficult to have patience. I was impatient to see what reaching fifty would reveal to me, as I did not then recognise that I was already on my spiritual path. My inner knowing did but not me. It may seem odd to separate the two out but that has been the only way to recognise what exists. The spirit in me is separate from my mind and body yet the same spirit is part and parcel of the universal spirit, the knowing. This distancing of myself from my mind and body was something I was able to do easily. It was as though I was naturally born with it and it is just a matter of accessing it, getting to understand it and be in contact with it. I was able to stand outside myself and witness my mind and body, proving I was more than either.

I first got a sense of witnessing when I walked past our local church one day, I felt as though I was inside an army tank and looking out the tiny slit window onto the world. I recognised I had this feeling before, I often felt apart from people and situations that surrounded me and thought I must be the odd one out. When I later found out witnessing is a valuable part of meditation I was very relieved and was easily able to build on what I had already experienced.

I could recognise the same knowing that was expressed in the books that I read, I could see it in the spiritual teachers I saw. It was like the knowing inside me acknowledging the knowing that exists in others. A deep inner knowing connection, it is as though we are all plugged into the same wiring system.

As I was reading The Power of Now by Eckhart Tolle for the first time I became aware of the spaces between each printed word on the page. As I really looked at those spaces they seemed more important than the words. In those spaces existed a vast stillness and that stillness was filled with silence. I connected. It is by experiencing such a connection that you know it exists. Someone could tell you over and over again, you might believe them as they are an honest person or some authority on the subject but to really 'know' you must experience it for yourself. That leaves no doubt in your mind. Of course many people would chose to argue otherwise but because you know, there is no need for you to prove that you are right. I always liked a story about a monk who was faced with an argumentative person who wanted to find fault in his spirituality. The monk turned to him and asked did he want a five or ten minute argument. Arguing for arguments sake, that person wanted to prove a point not learn.

I did not want to dispute spiritual teachers I wanted to learn from them. I was prepared to sit at their feet and just listen, be open to what I was hearing. I heard my first spiritual teacher when I was eighteen and I knew that what he was saying was right. It was Krishnamurti who was speaking at his school in Hampshire, it was the first time I had seen or heard a Swami speak. It was about things that I have never heard spoken about before yet they felt good to hear. The knowing that existed within me connected to it and said 'ah yes', this is what I have been waiting to hear. I carried the words of the spiritual teacher with me for nearly thirty years to the point where I wanted to awaken the spirituality that lay within myself. That inner knowing deep within myself had the wisdom and patience to wait until the time was right for me to develop the spiritual side of myself.

There is the deep instinctual type of knowing and there is a more surface kind of intellectual knowing, the reasoning part of the brain that likes to know all the answers. On a spiritual path it is best to remain open to the unknown, to be open to new experiences and sensations. To try and not reason them out but to accept them as just sensations and feelings, to trust the process that all will be revealed to you in time. It is also okay not to know. I have found that the more I have studied the more I come to the conclusion that I know nothing. Nothingness is okay too. Spirituality is not something to learn, it is something to realise that it exists within yourself. It is always already there for you to discover, you do not have to be clever to be spiritual. In many ways the intellect can hinder your progress, trying to reason everything out, it only creates a blockage to your connection. If you can breathe you can connect, it is that easy.

It was through following my breath in guided exercises that I got my taste of the essence of spirituality. Breath is God given and natural, without it we would die but we take it for granted, we depend on air for life. Our bodies automatically inhale and exhale without us being involved in the process. If you bring your attention to breathing in and out you can become aware of the subtlety of the process. Our whole body expands and contracts with the breath and through meditation you can become aware of the whole universe contracting and expanding at the same time. It is as though the universe is breathing for you. ' What a ridiculous statement' you might say, 'I do my own breathing not the universe' but just be open to that possibility. Do not analyse it, just try it, give it a go and see what happens. There is a slight internal shift to another dimension. Be like a visitor, visit it and return. If it feels right you can visit again, it will always be there waiting for you.

In some ways I see meditation a bit like space travel, I visit different spaces of expanding awareness. Often when I get there I think to myself this feels good and want to return to it. Perhaps this is a simplified version of what happens but it is not what many people think meditation is. It is not a trance like state, it is a beautiful serenity that one enters. The experience can differ from person to person so I cannot say what someone else might experience, only what I do. There are no laid down guidelines, do this and so and so will happen. If it was that easy more people would be enlightened but we are not talking as enlightenment as a goal. It is more of a personal spiritual development that can be achieved, not some ideal that you think is for other people not yourself. Yet if you want to progress on your spiritual path you have to regularly practice.

Chapter 3

Meditation

There are moments in one's daily life when you unknowingly enter a timeless space. You only realise that you have been somewhere when you come out of it and you are not quite sure where that was. Beautiful music, pleasant surroundings or similar opportunities can allow us to naturally drop into that timeless space.

Meditation to me means entering the timeless space that already exists and is a way of reconnecting to it. We had the natural ability to do it when we were babies and young children but over the years we lose that connection. It is always there, we just become disconnected and it gets covered over by our daily lives. Life is full of physical and mental activity and that seems to take priority. A human being is described as having a mind, body and soul. The first two are easily acknowledged but the third is often ignored, perhaps only resurfacing when one is faced with a life crisis.

I came to meditation because I wanted to reconnect with my soul. I had been very fortunate that I have a family and a good life with little financial worries. The term comfortably off would spring to mind, I lacked nothing; enjoyed most material pleasures, good holidays etc. However, deep down within me there was a hollow feeling where I felt 'there must be more to life than this'. Gaining a new desired material object would turn to ashes in my hand and I was disappointed at the lack of satisfaction it would bring, a fleeting feeling of pleasure at gaining it then that feeling was gone. The hopes of what the object would bring were short lived and it did not enhance my life as I thought it would. The old adage of 'wanting' is better than 'having', rang true. The empty feeling within me could not be satisfied with accruing material possessions nor could it be satisfied by continual activity or socialising.

A busy life meant a busy mind and like many people who come to meditation I was looking for the off button. It is never that simple, meditation initially involved concentration. The breath is used as an ideal vehicle on which to focus one's mind. By focusing the mind in this way it allows timeless space to reveal itself to you. By regular practice of meditation timeless space becomes more apparent and its restful peace felt. Once you get a taste for it, it helps to maintain the momentum of your daily practice. Practice is needed for improvement and an initial personal commitment is needed in the early stages, say ten minutes a day to start with. It is best to start small and gradually build on your practice. There is no point in expecting yourself to sit quietly in the early stages for an hour, fidgeting and fretting that one is unable to quieten one's mind. Meditation is not about pressurising or punishing yourself. The old habits that once ran your life have to be looked at with fresh eyes to see that they are outmoded.

Meditation is a gift to yourself, to allow yourself to be truly free from all your life's constraints even it is just for a short while. Those big heavy bags of life's concerns can be placed at your feet before you sit down to meditate. They have no place in meditation practice and it is your personal choice to let them interfere with your practice or not.

In meditation it is too easy to sabotage your practice and this is where a teacher helps in identifying and dealing with difficulties. Too often the mind plays tricks, telling us 'that it's boring' or 'we'll never get the hang of it'. There could be a nagging little voice at the back of one's mind saying 'you will never be any good at this, why bother?' Once these mind games have been clearly seen, there is the choice of listening to them or not.

The mind is determined to remain in control and has no wish to lose its control over you. It is going to play mind games and keep its continual activity going. I found, in the early days of meditation that as soon as I sat down to meditate my mind would run here and there, reliving recent scenarios, making shopping lists, daydreaming – anything but meditating. With practice this mind activity can be overcome and the true benefits of meditation reaped.

With practice, the mind activity decreases and the peaceful timeless space increases. Silence and stillness become your soul mates. They are the balm that soothes and nurtures the soul. Too often we only become aware of silence in old churches but silence surrounds us all the time. All noise arises out of silence and goes back into it. Meditation allows a reconnection to the all-pervading silence that exists around us. It is there for the taking, it is not necessary to go off to a quiet spot, you can connect anywhere at any time. The silence exists beneath all sounds and it is waiting for you. Once you tune into silence more regularly you can become aware of the stillness that is conjoined with silence. Both feed the soul.

Meditation does not belong to any one particular religion but encompasses all. In a meditative state, you can feel the unity of all living creatures and plants on the planet. There is no separation between yourself and the universe, you are part of the whole. As your sense of connectedness develops, your outer body seems to dissolve and there is no physical separation between you and the whole, an inner harmony develops and that connection feels complete.

With meditation, one should not set out with expectations but it is human nature to do so, to always seek results. It needs a change of perception to allow meditation to reveal itself to you, allowing its secrets to be unfolded to you gradually. Time and patience are on your side, sit back and enjoy the ride.

I often liken meditation to space travel, I go to places I have never been before, I experience sensations I have never experienced before. It is a journey into the unknown, yet known, it is a return to a place of belonging. It differs from space travel in that it is not an outer journey but an inwards one, to the very core essential part of oneself. A very precious and beautiful core, that exists within each and every one of us. It is worth every effort made just to get in touch with that essence. To know it exists and to experience its awe and wonder is truly uplifting.

Once that connection is made and there can be varying degrees of that connection, you will wish to maintain that contact through meditation. This same connection can be realised in every day activities by bringing your attention to what you are doing. Simple tasks like cleaning, done with attention and awareness can help with your connectedness. Meditation starts with sitting quietly but soon spreads throughout your everyday life, it does not have to be confined to a set time and place.

It helps you to see the world around you in a new light, to find a child's delight at the everyday objects that were taken for granted. A richness in the normality of life can be discovered. Fascination can be found on light refracted in a raindrop or the softness of a newly formed leaf. Nature gives an abundance of sensory living things for our enjoyment. Through meditation I have found the ability to stop, pause and look at things, I ponder in wonder at their having been created with such detail and imagination; the stars in the galaxy at night down to the hairy legs of a butterfly. It is positively awesome at what exists alongside us in nature, it is there for our pleasure if we want to enjoy it. Meditation has helped to improve my senses; my eyes seek out the details, my nose catches an aroma on the breeze, my ears can hear far off sounds, my taste buds are more alive and I enjoy the sensation of touching things anew. What a blessing and something I never expected to receive from meditation.

One of my hopes from learning meditation would be that my intuition would improve. It has been buried deep under the clouds of thoughts in my head. By clearing those clouds and creating an empty space, my intuition could rise to the surface once more. I have become very attached to the words beginning with 'i'. Increases in my inspiration, imagination, initiative; I hope will be the gains. Of course one of the pit falls in meditation is end gaining, hoping to achieve something from it. If you set yourself the goal of a clear mind it will elude you. There could be a multitude of other goals hoped for calm under stressful situations, decrease in fear, a happier disposition – the list is endless and personal. Just do not set them as goals or outcomes; otherwise they will never come to fruition. In the end they will occur and you will notice small differences in your life that can be built on. You are not going to wake up one day and all your problems will be eliminated. Meditation is like a silent mist seeping into your life, when the mist clears you realise that change has taken place and you personally had done nothing to bring it about except meditate.

In many respects it is best not to restrict meditation to the confines of sitting quietly but that is where it starts. Then it can go onto opening up a whole new perspective to one's life. It is an enriching process that can have no limitations. Simple revelations filter into everyday life, often imperceptibly and slowly your life tunes in with the wholeness of existence. You begin to feel more complete as you acknowledge and feed the soul. It becomes the re-found link in the mind, body and soul of a person. It links the individual part of us all to the universal and with it the realisation that there is no separation between them. We are all part and parcel of the whole.

Chapter 4

The heart

Much of my early work in meditation was to do with my heart chakra and I was encouraged to work on opening it out. Somehow over the years I had put a protective shell around it. I needed to find out why I had done so. This has been ongoing work, no miracle cures offered here. The more I worked on it, the harder I found the shell and that in itself has been a journey of discovery.

Perhaps it might be easier to start at this moment of writing and work back. I had come away from meditating hoping to find guidance on my path and felt nothing had come out of it. I started working on the computer then got waylaid, put on a CD of my favourite music from 'The Piano', a beautiful haunting piece. Before I knew it I was sobbing my heart out, I was reminded of my dream and hope of passion in my life. That daytime dream of a young girl who always thought her prince charming would come along and sweep her off her feet kind. It was much more than a superficial story line, it was a deep longing within me that had gone unanswered. I had longed for passion in my life, the sort that can transform and let miracles happen. Passion as a raw state of emotion, it was the hunger of the soul. In my younger teenage mind it was mainly associated with someone you loved deeply but now I realise its wider connotations.

At eighteen I met and fell in love with the man of my dreams. He was all that I wished for but he came with a whole sack full of problems. I innocently thought love could conquer all but I was wrong, the problems were insurmountable. I discovered very early on in our relationship that I was too young to cope with so many problems, my only choice was to let him go. Of course we didn't want to part but I could foresee that the problems would destroy our relationship anyway. It was a no win situation and that the best thing would be to end it earlier rather than later. One of the hardest things to do is to let someone go who you love deeply and truly believe that you were to spend the rest of your life with. From the moment fate brought us to together, when we fell in love at first sight, I believed it would be forever.

I loved him passionately and cried endlessly, at the hopelessness of the situation then. I thought I would never love again and never in that way. So at eighteen unbeknown to me I started to put the first layer of protective shell around my heart. I was determined that no man would ever hurt me to that depth again.

I was shocked at the sudden appearance of these feelings, I thought I had buried them and just got on with living my life. Over thirty years later I did not expect the feelings to be so fresh. It was the passion of the music I was listening to that linked to the passion of my youth and hence triggered painful memories. Yet it was during meditation they surfaced as a bubble being emitted from the depth of a pond and floated up to the surface of my consciousness. This bubble being released from the dark corners of my memory wished expression, I cried, I sobbed, I felt the vice grip around my heart as though the pain was too much to bear. The feelings deepened, heart rendering sobs that heaved my body, wide mouth sobs that emitted all the pain through my mouth and throat. It was as though my heart wanted to exhume all the pain that was trapped inside me. All that I have trapped in my heart wanted to break free from the snare I had imposed on it. As I continued to sob my body became lighter and freer, it was as though a weight had been lifted from me.

There is a sense that these negative feelings will never trouble me again, in the daylight of reasoning, they have been evaporated by the sun of consciousness. I was a mature woman now, had formed loving relationships but at the same time I wanted these to expand and develop not to be trapped in old thought forms and habits. Meditation had provided a safe environment for this release. It was not something I had set out to do, it just occurred naturally. It was an issue that needed freeing, if I was to move on and grow. The hopes and dreams we have can form chains around the heart and I no longer desired to be held down by them. It limited the way I related to people, it was based on past behaviour patterns. I wanted to be able to meet each fresh face with an openness of a new being and not have past memories restricting my communications. I wanted to be open to new possibilities and not shut off alternative avenues of interaction. Old thought forms, beliefs and habits can ensnare which allow no room for personal growth.

Meditation has taught me to be open, to be available to what is and welcome the unexpected. My old notions, ideas and views have to be reviewed, to question - are they working? Are they useful? Becoming aware that are they can be restrictive or even debilitating. Insecurities and lack of confidence had so often stopped what I would have liked to have done. My courage failed and there was no energy to carry forward my hopes or convictions. Letting go the ties of the past, surrendering to the present, the future would take care of itself; was my desired aim. I want to see each day, person and situation anew with innocent eyes.

The heart can be helped to heal by reassessing old habits and tendencies in this way, to come to terms if they are working or not. By doing so and coming to one's own conclusion allows change to happen. Saying no to out dated behaviour, feelings or emotions makes space for new ones to enter, it creates a gap for something more rewarding and in that space consciousness is able to flood.

In my unconscious awareness, I knew my heart had an outer casing around it, yet I would never admit it was I who put it there. In the same way I knew unconsciously that shell had to be broken. A sledgehammer to crack it would never have worked because I had constructed that shell for a very good reason. Over my lifetime I did not want to feel that original raw pain again so I had no incentive to break that shell.

It was through meditation I realised I had constructed that shell for my protection. At first I questioned what it was there for and why. Then I came to the realisation that I did not want the shell to be around my heart, it was hindering my spiritual path. This was all contained in the moments of my sobbing, through the pain came the realisation it was blocking my spiritual path and had to be removed if I was to progress. I had a choice to leave it there and remain stuck or remove it and carry on. I did not need to be blown away by this discovery because this came to the light of my awareness in a safe situation, I could deal with it.

My guru often told me I would only be given that which I could cope with and through meditation I was able to deal with the past memories and let them go. In this way I was able to let go of the past and its hold on me. Many similar experiences have arisen in this manner and I have chosen to bid them a fond farewell as they are no longer needed. I now welcome past negative events to be relived in this manner, as by clearing the debris of my past, I am freer and more open to the new.

In the empty spaces that are left I hope to allow my intuition to expand, my initiative to increase, my imagination to fly. I hope to tap into the passion felt in my youth and use it in its many guises, painting, music, gardening, dancing. Using that raw energy to be creative. I want to expand, to grow spiritually with an open heart. It has been thanks to my gurus who have taught and shown me how to open my heart more.

Chapter 5

Why a guru

Why have a guru, I would sum it up in two words, for inspiration and aspiration. A guru is someone who had trod the path before you and is established in the Consciousness. When I come into the presence of a true guru I can feel their energy field, I can look into their eyes and see eternity. They would never advertise this fact, you have to find it out for yourself and recognise it. A guru acts as a signpost to lead the way but you always need to look beyond the person. When they talk their words and actions can inspire you and you get a new feeling arising within you, aspiration; that with effort you too could achieve what they have achieved. They make it clear that it is within your own capabilities if you put your whole being into it, it is not something just for them, it is available to all and they are here you help you get there.

Their guidance is invaluable; they understand human failings and fragility, trying to show ways around or through problems. They are not outside this world but live within it, they are part of the human race and have a deep understanding of it. It is a wonderful opportunity to benefit from their guidance. Often it is just enough to sit in their presence and your questions will be answered, what passes between guru and pupil can be beyond words. You can learn by just being with them. Practicalities do exist, practices do need to be suggested and various reading material proffered but ultimately it is up to you to do the practice, it is your own personal journey not theirs. You cannot expect them to do the hard work for you while you sit back and a wise guru makes this very clear.

A spiritual path is a difficult one to follow and it does need practice to stay on it and achieve insight. It is a human fault to avoid practice and for me it was the same. I could easily say I would practice every day but doing it every day was another matter. I could always find a good excuse for not doing it; I had housework or gardening. Or I would think it is so boring, I would prefer reading a book; anything other than sitting quietly and meditating. It took a lot of will power to overcome all my arguments for not practicing. A guru's advice just to go and sit at the same place at the same time was a start and then I could build on it; this is what I did. It was like training a recalcitrant puppy, I had to be told and made to do it by myself. Slowly over time I got used to it and as my meditation practice improved and as I gained its benefits, I was willing to practice more often. When a guru started his practice he would have had similar difficulties, he knows what works and would not, so a pupil can reap from his past experience.

It takes a lifetime's work to create the special energy field a guru has, I can only describe it as peaceful. I just 'am' in their presence, with no agitation or no racing mind, it feels so restful. Coming into their energy field of peace I feel like a purring cat that wants to rub round their legs for pleasure. To sit at the feet of a master is enough and a guru would humbly accept your thanks, as he/she would see it as the Consciousness, which filters through him/her. A true guru would never seek disciples, yes people do come and they are willing to share their gifts but they never set out or advertise the fact. Hence true gurus are not easy to find. It is said that if a guru and pupil are meant to learn together, they will meet unplanned and that has often been the case for me. It was a natural coming together as though it was always meant to be, yet at the same time I could never have envisaged it happening.

On first meeting a guru there is an inner connection, which is hard to define, I recognise something so special within them that I want within me. You know that what exists within them can also exist within yourself, something so special it defies being put into words. Each person has an inner 'knowing', a guru knows all about 'knowing' and can put you back in touch with it. It is beyond the mind and thinking, beyond a gut instinct but a guru understands it and can help a pupil to be more at home with it.

I have found contentment in just sitting in a guru's presence; the silence is a powerful learning tool. Too often words take one away from the silence, the silence can contain the answers you need to know. Knowing is found only in the silence. Of course there are moments when questions have to be asked but I often find I do not need to directly ask them as by listening to a guru talk the questions answer themselves.

It is a joy, to listen to a guru speak to a group of listeners. By keeping your ears and mind open, much needed advice and guidance can be received. I recently attended a Guru Puja (thanks to the guru) day at a nearby ashram, where a visiting swami was giving a talk. He clearly understood the problems that occurred in daily life with work and family, he knew of the stones and boulders that obscure ones path and could help with their removal. When you listen to talks there are often repeated themes, which you have heard before but sometimes you hear them with fresh ears and it hits home. Something clicks inside you and you really understand what has been said, for the first time. There is recognition of the truth of his words and their relevance reverberates within you, you get that 'I know feeling'. There are times when I might question if I just have a vivid imagination but I know this not to be the case. It all goes back to the inner 'knowing' that exists within you.

A guru provides the coming home to beauty. In everyday life we get desensitised to the beauty that exists all around us. A guru can put us back in touch with this beauty and also the beauty that is within us. A guru wants to share this beauty with others and for them in turn to share their own beauty, it is not something to remain hidden but openly shared and can have a knock on effect. Beauty is accessible to each of us, it is within every breath we breathe and it feels good. It is just a matter of accessing it and meditation greatly aids this. The light in a guru's eyes can touch your heart, their eyes can shine with a visible inner joy and you say yes to yourself, I want some of that.

The first swami I came into close contact with ran an ashram locally, of which there are few in U.K. I had heard all about ashrams in India and had always dreamed that perhaps one day I would go and stay there. I had never been brave enough to go there so I was very fortunate to have the soft option and go to one in this country. My new yoga teacher at the time used to go there for the monthly satsang (coming together and giving thanks) and asked if I would like to join her. It came as quite a shock to walk in on the fire ceremony for the first time and it seemed I had stepped into a completely different culture. The swami explained the fire ceremony and its significance as we went through it and I began to appreciate its delicacy and beauty as a way of giving thanks.

The resident swami who presides over the ceremony is now in his eighties and a true adherent of yoga. He lives the ascetic life of a swami, following the ancient teachings closely – he is an inspiration to those who follow yoga, and he can still perform all the yogic postures with agility and strength. He has a slight and wiry build, which belies the strength of many a younger man. His spiritual practice is his life; diet and cleansing are all closely followed. He welcomes those who respect the spiritual life to join him at the ashram. He has lived and worked in the outside world and helped to raise a family, whilst yoga has been his life. He does not deviate from the original teaches in the Bhagvad Gita and I can admire such dedication.

It was only when I did some karma yoga at the ashram that we got to know each other better, up till that time I think I were wary. In the initial stages I never knew how to respond to a swami, I was quite happy to just listen and speak when only spoken too. As my confidence has grown in spiritual matters I have been able to approach them more easily. When I was given the opportunity of carrying out karma yoga at the ashram I went to stay there for four days. Normally when you stay there you have to adhere to the routine of the ashram but as I had my work cut out repainting it, I was excused most of it. Meals are taken in silence but afterwards I had the opportunity of conversing with the swami and we came to a closer understanding of each other. The swami wears white robes, choosing not to wear the expected orange ones. He lives quietly and alone following humbly the pursuit of yoga. As he says an ashram is not made of brick and mortar it is made from the vibrations of the people that attend them. He is someone to whom I can aspire to and I admire his dedication to the cause of yoga. How fortunate I am to have such an oasis close by.

Some swamis were not so nearby and I had to travel to Spain to meet my next two. They were a married couple that taught energy enhancement and yoga in Spain and Argentina. I still marvel today that I trod into the unknown by going out to join them on my own to Spain. I think my mother thought it might be some weird sect that I would never return from, it was a risk I was prepared to take but I must say I was on the alert for anything too unusual. I was having problems at the time before going and felt my spiritual path was wandering and needed fresh input. I plunged in with both feet and booked two weeks with them, not knowing exactly what to expect. I went with the sole intention of learning and when the swami asked why I had come, my reply was 'to learn' and learn I did.

Only when I was out there did I realise the convoluted route that had brought me there and that it must have been meant to be all along. It started when computers first became cheaply available that I had one and was able to link onto the Internet. First stop was yoga and meditation websites. I was amazed at the amount and variety and wondered how I could possibly choose one. After dipping into quite a few I was drawn to a Kundalini yoga site and registered on it. I used to receive many interesting talks and useful practices through friendly informative emails. They followed all the major yoga principles and kept my thoughts on the higher concepts with a daily bulletin of 'food for thought'. I cannot emphasis how useful this was on keeping me on my path. At the time I used to only attend one yoga class a week and was busy raising a family but just with that one thought I could focus on each day, greatly helped.

I remained totally unaware that their website was infiltrated by another, I thought it was just a change of name, as the ideas remained the same. Little did I know the swami in Spain was also a computer whiz, so I started enjoying his site unbeknown to me. He is a well read and knowledgeable man who enthusiastically puts his ideas across in an easily digestible form. I always read all that was emailed to me and was fascinated by participants' testimonials, they all seemed very genuine. It became obvious that for any one attending his courses things happened and I was ready to make things happen for me. But what of the man himself, I was not able to gain an impression of him until videos could be sent on the Internet and I was able to hear his voice for the first time. There was a solidity and strength to his voice that I found soothing, it had a depth to it I could trust. With that surmise I headed off to Spain to meet him and his wife, which shall be covered in a later chapter.

Undoubtedly the most important guru in my life has been the guru who introduced me formally to meditation and later to sounding and sanskrit. It was at the same ashram that I first heard him speak, all that he spoke of connected to my inner 'knowing'.

Chapter 6

Guru

Where can I start talking about my guru when there seems no beginning or end to our meeting? It is more like a 'coming home' than a 'getting to know another person'. Inside I have always felt 'different', perhaps this is because I never expressed it to others but when speaking with my guru I knew he understood fully what I felt inside.

By forty-five my children were becoming more independent and I had space for myself. What did I do? I filled the gap with activity, doing all the things I imagined they had stopped me doing over the years. I maintained a wide network of family and friends as well as making new friendships through the village fundraising and voluntary work that I did. I wanted to feel needed and valued and this was the route I took to get my needs met but somehow there still remained an unanswered gnawing inside me, which I could not so easily fulfil.

It has only been through getting to know and trust my guru that this need is being resolved. He has been the portal to the universal consciousness that I instinctively always knew existed. I did not intend having a guru, I am sceptical by nature and need to test the water thoroughly before I jump in. It's not a belief system; it's an inward knowing that exists. It's a matter of choosing to access, or not. It's all experiential, only believe something when you have felt it and that is an excellent guiding rule. It's not about being told something with conviction, you have to feel it for yourself and then you will know. Explaining how you know is not easy to do, it's more of a gut feeling that has a meaning all of its own. The more you acknowledge these feelings, the more you can become used to them and can learn from them. I am still learning and will expect to do so for the rest of my life. In one respect this opened my life out from its narrow confines and released me to be available to the unknown. It is being prepared to accept the unknown and live with it. Not just grab hold of a comfortable and tested view on life in order to feel secure.

My guru and I have made a long journey together, I may lightly skip over many important happenings and be selective in what I present but it all adds up to the whole. He has guided my life from the beginnings of a spiritual path to the present time. Deep down I now know it was a path that always awaited me. I am not sure if the path came to me or I went on the path. Looking back I understand I was on the path all the time, I just did not know it. Part of my reasoning for writing this book is to encourage others but also make sense of my own spiritual path. Each and every one of us has a spiritual path; it's not just for the selected few. At some quiet point in your life, fall quiet listen to the space and silence that surrounds you, be brave enough to look inside yourself. Is your soul there waiting to meet you? Have a go now, don't put off till tomorrow, do it now.

I would label myself as 'normal', as if that was something to aspire to. I blend in with the crowd, am family minded and happily mix with all races. However, I am far from being so called 'normal', I am different. But I have kept that difference to myself for fear of being ostracised, now it is time to stand up and be counted and you the reader can form your own opinions.

On initially seeing my guru, he looked far from normal. His unkempt wayward hair, which he brushes from his face, gave him a heathen look. He was a well-built man heading for sixty yet remained totally oblivious as to his appearance. I have yet to met a person who is so non materialistic either in dress or possessions. I can just hear him say, when he reads this, 'I never realised I looked that bad' – which proves my point. We have a good rapport, which contains humour and laughter. It has taught me to look beyond the superficial and it's been a good lesson for life, not to go by appearance but look toward the real person that exists beneath. Immediately I was struck by the colour and depth of his pale blue eyes. I have never seen eyes like it, it was as though they were not of this world at all. They pierced right through me and there was no hiding place. Since then in special moments I have see them as a faceted diamond, each facet refracting spectrums of coloured light.

I first met my guru when I went to a nearby ashram to hear him talk. I went with my yoga teacher and a few of our group. His reputation had preceded him and I was eager to hear what he had to say. I wasn't disappointed but it was early days for me, much of what he said went over my head but other parts resonated with me. It was more the way he spoke that I was drawn to, the softness in his voice, the beauty with which he pronounced the words. By hearing him I knew what he was talking about was real and not some vague concept. His presence exuded a depth of being that went far beyond a physical body. He was and is a learned man of intelligence and wisdom and I have been eternally grateful for his patience and guidance over the years.

Our relationship developed through my yoga teacher who'd known him through a school of meditation that they'd both been aligned. She was familiar with his thinking and outlook, as well as respecting his depth of knowledge and being. It was only when I moved house to another village that I found this yoga teacher, after several ineffective tries at other teachers. I enjoyed her method of teaching yoga, which allowed a spiritual awareness to enter. In relaxation and silent moments, there was an opportunity to get in contact with the still dimension that exists within us. She was a close follower of Jean Klein and had attended his seminars and retreats in this country in the past. She was able to share her spiritual studies of Advaita and formed a study group locally. This opened my eyes to the many books that were available on the subject as she had gathered together a small library from which we were able to freely borrow.

In our study group, she would bring up for discussion suitable extracts from relevant books to deepen our understanding. Never before had I come into contact with these writings. In the first place I would never have known what to look or even ask for. It has taken a lot of trial and error out of my reading. If a particular book did not resonate, I could try another, at no expense or effort on my part. Besides the established works such as the Bhagavad Gita and Upanisads, there were more up-to-date writings of Jean Klein, Eckhart Tolle etc. It was from the background I was able to approach my guru, to clarify what was contained within them.

My guru regularly came to our small group to give guided mediations and talks. I also came into closer contact with him on the occasional retreats that were organised at a nearby convent. The first one I attended, I remember driving there, I wondered what I was letting myself in, quite prepared to turn the car home and forget all about it, but I didn't and the rest is history, as they say.

On first meeting my guru there was a connection but in another way I was sceptical, so I kept my distance and watched. We met up on retreats, talks and visits to our local study group. As my trust in him grew I felt able to approach him concerning personal problems and ways of using my spiritual practices to cope with them. This is where he came into his own. My main concern at the time was that my father had cancer of the prostate and bones, a long drawn out illness of much pain and suffering. I felt inadequate to ease his pain and it was hard to stand by and watch it. My guru really listened to what I had to say whilst giving practical advice on how best to deal with the situations, suggesting particular spiritual practices, which would help. Other deaths followed, my son's depression, miscellaneous relationship problems; I could express my concerns openly in his non-judgemental presence. Things I hadn't been able to utter before were able to flow from my lips. I could freely shed the bottled up tears and every time it was as though a weight had been lifted from my shoulders after speaking to him. The practices he suggested I utilised and they helped me deal with many a difficult situation. In this way they were proved to be effective and beneficial. If I had any concerns he would was there to give guidance. Those sessions spent with him were very special to me, I felt protected and cared for. At the end of them we naturally embraced before parting, no more words needed to be said. I dissolved into his presence and it felt good. There were no longer two people standing in a room, they had disappeared into something more unifying. I struggle to find the right description to portray it, as it is indescribable, you only just know.

As I shared more of myself with him, I began to trust him more. I felt at ease with him and from that time onwards a deep and lasting relationship has flourished. Of course it's not always been as easy going as it might first appear. I am not the kind of person to be told what to do, or to hero-worship any one, so disagreements naturally arose. I have learnt to speak openly and directly to him about difficult subjects, not to let emotions run away with me and not to hide unwanted feelings. I dropped all the defensive mechanisms that I had used in the past and he provided me with a safe environment in which to do so. I am now able to identify false behaviour patterns that have not worked for me and to make changes. To change is a slow drawn out process, there is no simple route or magic wand. More often than not, it is painful and no one wants to suffer pain. Sometimes I have to give myself a strong silent telling off, as though to a recalcitrant child, that I have to grit my teeth and get on and do it, in order to reap the benefits.

Meditation has enabled me to slowly change, no miracles over night just steady subtle movements forward, which are hardly noticeable at first. At times it seems as though nothing has moved, then something happens and you realise you have changed. My son was recently eating his dinner in the lounge and using BBQ sauce, he gave it a good shake not realising the top was loose. It went all over the pale yellow carpet and settee. I walked in and saw it without a flicker of emotion and placidly cleared it up, before I would have become irate. 'Wow' I thought this is great. I was tired of the continual irritation that arises through a family environment, it's as though it's a breeding ground for them. I don't want to get annoyed over triviality which, in the great scheme of things, are of no importance. I longed for a constant even temperament. That doesn't mean to say emotions do not arise but it's more a case of appropriately arising connected with the situation presented at the time, not just an accumulation of stress. It is no use sitting in a quiet forest or convent thinking you'd got it; the test lies in living with people and when you can do that and still keep the quietude, you definitely know you've made it.

I think it is a misconception to think enlightenment is for the select few monks or Buddha's. It is available to all that seek it. It is no easy path to follow and I've just tentatively put my feet on its beginning, whilst at the same time thinking I'm not up to this. But what have I got to lose compared to what I could gain? Meditation is all about practice, I initially thought I couldn't maintain a practice every day but before I knew it, there I was. It first started with my yoga when I gave up the class. I thought I could never get up every morning and do an hour's practice. I started with ten minutes on occasional days, this filtered into every day, then the time of practice increased and eventually I ended up doing yoga every day for an hour. The same has happened with my meditation practice. I released myself from goal setting and the goal arrived. Now if I don't practice I miss it and my body and mind feel its lack. It soon reaped numerous benefits that have become part of my life.

Too many things have been just plain hard work in my life, quite a slog in fact with very little to do with enjoyment; even when sometimes they first appeared pleasurable. So my criterion with yoga and meditation was to enjoy it and give up trying to achieve. If benefits came my way, well and good, I was not going to seek them out, I would just practice.

Quietening the mind for meditation seemed impossible at first as my mind was incessantly on the go – replaying conversations and events, thinking, imaging, dreaming. Sometimes I felt I lived in my mind more than the physical world. I came to a point when I thought, I have had enough of this, I would like a quiet empty mind and that was how I came to meditation.

My guru has given me numerous techniques to learn and try, but persistence is the name of the game. Initially one has to be proactive in ones practice, it's not just a matter of sitting quietly hoping it will happen. I have been hesitant about teaching meditation as I did not think people realised practice is needed if you want to succeed. It's not enough to go to a class once a week and think 'oohh' that was nice, practice is needed every day if things are going to change. Say if you want to be good at a sport, you need to practice at every opportunity the same applies to meditation. How it differs is that you take trying out of the equation and just leave the doing.

I took this same philosophy when I decided to learn Sanskrit, I wonder did I really choose it or did it come to me. Years back my teacher predicted I would learn it and I looked at him in disbelief – 'no way' was my response. I have never been able to learn foreign languages easily and what looked like hieroglyphics seemed impossible. As time passed and I listened to its sound, I liked it. Certain words I was drawn to and I liked them in particular for no reason. It was by asking my teacher their meaning that I realised their significance, they did have a special relevance to me. The sound carries the meaning so that you instinctively know what is meant. It works on such a subtle level, which seems beyond comprehension, that you just have to trust it. It's as if by some miracle, the feeling evolves that there is a greater force out there working.

As I sat at the first Sanskrit class, I thought to myself 'I would never get the hang of this'. I don't know if it was my age or hormones but my memory is poor. You can tell me one thing and I've forgotten it the next, it didn't bode well for learning Sanskrit. It took me back to schooling and struggling with my lessons with an unsympathetic teacher standing over me. My Sanskrit teacher was very different; kind, patient and understanding putting no pressure at all on the learning process. The onus was on the pupil to learn, web sites could provide the basics of grammar and we were to seek them out ourselves. That left the class free to focus on the oral teaching of the great works. The joy in this method is hearing the words pronounced perfectly first hand. If you put learning aside and just listen to the sounds made, they have a beauty all of their own. The intonations flow and the softness of emphasis leaves you marvelling. I was determined to find the enjoyment in learning Sanskrit and put aside any negativity I had about my learning abilities.

Just when I began to think I would never progress, something moved and learning became a little easier. At the point of writing I would say I am slowly remembering the sanskrit alphabet and am able to write down the letters and pronounce them from memory. I can also painfully read aloud. I marvel at my teacher's patience with me at the mistakes I make. I squirm and he finds them endearing.

He encourages me not to put myself down, it took him 35 years of hard study to get where he is, and he reminds me I could not hope to pick it up in a short time. How fortunate I am to have such an understanding teacher, this way of learning is a far cry from the memories I had of my schooling.

Another obstacle I had to overcome was the sounding involved in Sanskrit. It has to be out loud and in a group. As a child I used to love singing until I got to secondary school when the music teacher wondered what that horrible noise was in her class. In front of my fellow pupils she identified it as me and offered singing lessons in the break. I was too embarrassed to go and stopped singing from that day forth, opting to mime instead. A door shut on the enjoyable pastime of singing for me, she could not have imagined the damage she did although she meant well at the time. So I got to the Sanskrit classes fearful on opening my mouth at the age of nearly fifty. With my teacher's natural ability to make you feel relaxed and not bother at what you sounded like, I was prepared to give it a go. Confidence grew with practice and I realised I didn't sound as bad as I thought I did. I shared my experiences with fellow students and most had similar experiences to mine. There I was thinking they'd got it sussed all along. Be open as you possibly can and share your feelings with others, you might be surprised at the outcome. You may have already lost self-esteem so you have little to lose, but by sharing you have much to gain and your fears can be quickly eliminated. Even if you got a blank stare back, the listener would go home at think about it, realising how brave you were to bring it up!

A side benefit on using my voice again was that when my son had a karaoke party for his 21st I was up there giving it my best. That did not mean I could suddenly sing but that I enjoyed the fun of singing again.

Chanting often seems easier than sounding, it is just like singing and lifts your spirits. It doesn't have to be precise, and it's just the joy of making a delightful noise. I have blended the two together and just get on with it. I have been pleasantly surprised at how good I feel after doing it, there is a spring in my step and a smile on my lips. As I practiced chanting the Sanskrit I noticed an enhancement in my moods after each session. With the sounding this has fed into my meditation, it prepares my mind for the quiet and being still.

A benefit of the sounding and chanting is that my speech has improved. I seem to be able to use my vocal tonal range to express myself better. The softness I hear in my teacher's voice, I try to incorporate in mine. It is a very caring way to speak instead of using harsh tones when talking to people. Notice the softness in your voice when you're talking to a baby, why does it have to change when talking to your spouse or a stranger?

I have complained to my guru that I couldn't possibly do all the practices he has given me, there would be no time left in the day for me to do the housework (not as though I want to do it). Pick and mix was his reply and I like that concept. Somehow if you are open you instinctively know what is the right practice for that day. Even if you got it wrong it would not matter. My guru has taught me so much, he is an encyclopaedia of spiritual and religious knowledge. He knows and can quote from Shakespeare and the Bible when relevant. He can teach so as I will listen and reflect on what is said but most of all he has shown me how meditation can be part of family life.

On one particular session with him I was pondering of what to do with my life. He simply asked "what do you really want to do?" instantaneously I replied 'I want to write more than anything'. It had been a long time dream that I had never made any move towards fruition, one of those dreams that had always got put on the back burner and suddenly because I was asked the question direct, it came up. Once it had come to my awareness in this way I was able to do something about it and that was to find a creative writing class. It just takes that initial step to start the walk. The experiences and friends I have made from that first step have been so rewarding. A dear friend I made from the first class is kindly editing this book for me and we exchange light hearted banter through emails regularly. At the same time she is coping with MS and all that entails but most of all she has started her meditation journey. It is a wonderful snowball effect that enriches your life beyond your widest imagination, just one decision.

My spiritual journey would not have come so far if it were not for my guru. His continual love and support have seen me through the difficult times and beyond them.

Chapter 7

Death

When I was discussing the subject of death with my guru, he looked into my eyes and said 'death will not part us', then asked if I understood this. I replied 'only vaguely'; I knew it in principle through what I had been studying but not in actual reality.

At the time of writing, within the last six months there have three deaths of family and friends. I pessimistically say they come in three, now. Over the past ten years there has been a long line of them. Up to that time I was able to keep death at an arms distance, people had died that I knew and cared about but no one really close to me had. It started with my grandmother, she was very fortunate to have lived a healthy life, until one day at 89 she felt unwell and dropped down dead in the bathroom, as a result of an aneurysm. It was the best kind of death one could wish for, no long drawn out period of illness and suffering, just to go quickly and silently as though stepping into another room. Death is that stepping into another room or space. It cannot be termed heaven or hell, as religions are prone to define it. It is a return to consciousness from which we came and can be very beautiful.

'How' you might wonder can I say this with conviction. I was having hypnosis for my skin condition when I underwent a near death experience. As usual I was sceptical about having hypnosis and thought myself to be an unlikely candidate but I was prepared to give it a try. When the hynotherapist said my arm would rise up, I thought to myself, 'you'll be lucky' but it rose by itself, much to my surprise. I try to be open to the unknown and unexplainable, therefore when the near death experience happened I did not label it as such. I told it to the hynotherapist and he just accepted what I said but made no comment. It was only years later when discussing it with other people that they named it as a near death experience.

All I can say it was something that had never happened to me before and was very powerful. A brilliant white light encompassed me. It was so awe-inspiring, magnificent and vivid in its luminosity; I struggle to find words good enough to describe it. What I felt in its aura was that it was calling me to it, a strong call that could not be resisted. Somehow I knew that I should not go with it. It ended and was gone; leaving me quite bewildered as to what had happened.

To gain a better understanding of it, I discussed it with a spiritual healer who said I could have actually gone with the call and it would have been alright, I would have come back. I still question 'would I have been able to take that risk?' The experience has shown me dying can be a beautiful experience but human fear gets in the way of experiencing that beauty.

I have since been able to see dead people and sit with them without any qualms. There is a facial serenity with no worry lines, all that remains is a peaceful countenance. This leaves one knowing they have gone to a better place. After years of suffering it can be a blessed release but to those left behind it is the beginning of coming to terms with losing a loved one.

I always wondered how a God could let people suffer so, and have never really been taken with the idea of a God and all that entails. God is what religions are made out of where different religions can fight each other. It goes to show that God can be created to fit separate moulds depending on the belief system involved. It leaves out universal love for the whole where a commonality needs to be found not separateness. We are all born and we all die, we share the same sun and moon. We breathe the same air, drink the same water and share the same space – these are good starting points.

Many cultures cannot share death; it is something to be kept hidden where feelings are not openly shown. Tears have to be shed behind closed doors. It's only at funerals where people come together in acknowledgement of death and that a communal recognition that life is transitory occurs. The funerals I've been to normally focus on the gift of life with thanks given for it. They look back over the person's life with gratitude that you were able to know them and be part of their life. The gift of life can be recognised when it is too late, when there is precious little left of it. There is a need for everyone to celebrate the gift of life everyday. No matter how bad the circumstances of it, good can always be found. It can be in the sound of a bird, the radiance of a flower, a warm breeze on your face. Each day we are showered by these gifts yet they go unnoticed.

Why wait till death calls to become aware of their preciousness? Nature surrounds us all the time and yet we have become immune to it. Accepting it to always be just there for us. Only in its' absence would its value be found. Just like when you are thirsty and water is scarce, you realise its importance. Death occurs naturally in nature, it is part of the life cycle, with little fuss about it. Each person has the opportunity to learn from nature if they choose. Life and death are the two side of the same coin.

When my Dad was in a hospice I always felt that if I could only wheel him outside he would feel better. The sunshine on his face would ease his pain or the wind in his hair would quell the side effects of the drugs; all that remained was his suffering. It was as though suffering had overtaken him and that was all that was left. All I could do was stand by and watch. When this got too much,

I would go outside to breathe the air and find release from the oppressive desolation. Hospices try to be cheerful places, where every comfort is given but they are places where death has to be stared directly in the face; for those in there and for those who visit. There is no let out clause, there is no hope of recovery.

As I write this I have just received via a cousin, one of those chain emails that remind you to value your life and friends. It told of a story of a grown man and the death of his childhood neighbour next door. He remembered him fondly for his help when he was a young boy, but as an adult never got the time to visit him. The long and short of the tale was the greatest gift you can give, is of your time before it is too late.

I tried to make sure I spent time with my father but I never felt it was enough. His face always lit up when he saw me, when he would make light of his illness. Humour was used many a time to cover awkward situations. There was an untold code that the unspeakable would never be mentioned, his forthcoming death. The rawness of death is so visible in a hospice when the person in the opposite bed dies in front of you. Screens put around cannot obscure the reality of what is happening and there is the knowing it will be your turn soon. That body wheeled away, the sobbing relatives. You know what will be happening after you are gone.

What I enjoyed most about my father was his sense of humour and fun. He had the ability to make people laugh. He could say the most outrageous things to strangers, whilst I would squirm with embarrassment, they would find it highly amusing and burst out laughing. I can smile back at the memory of those times. One of the things death teaches is to remember the good times and appreciate their value. Even small things that you overlooked as a child can come back to you, to be cherished in your memory again. My Dad was a motor mechanic and I would often help him in the evenings when he was doing a 'homer'. When my legs were long enough I could bleed the brakes for him. His garage was his life and after his death when I had to clear it out recently I wrote a piece about it for my creative writing class.

"I inhaled the air, which smelt of a cold musty engine room with grease that stuck like treacle to a spoon, my eyes caught the row of jars containing nuts and screws. I could hear the sound of grinding flour as my Dad opened a hopeful jar and the shaking out of screws onto a newspaper, landing like pinpricks of rain on glass. My father was known far and wide for the contents of his shed. If a neighbour needed a missing screw one would surely be found from his collection of jars on the shelf. Only he would be able to go straight to the necessary jar and discover an identical one. Along the shelves side were the collection of screws in jam jars with ones of nuts, bolts, nails, and washers. Jars standing like soldiers to attention in a row.

I quickly scooped the jars off their resting-place into large cardboard boxes I could hear the shattering of glass. Each slither digging into my heart. I kept telling myself history could not be contained in jars but I knew it was. When the shelves were bare I brushed away the thick black lace cobwebs. They were tacky with decay and tasted of bile, which clung like death to a corpse. Their acrid sooty smell assailed my nostrils and brought back memoirs of the chimney being swept as a child. I remembered the excitement when the brush appeared out of the top of the chimney and I always greeted it with glee. There were so many happy times to recall.

I stood beside my Dad's bench and ran my fingers across the cold metal surface, which felt like a used lead pipe. Smooth and undulating with a history of use, like walking through a darkened forest never knowing what was in store? Oil stains remained as puddles after the tide has gone out. The bench timber frame smelt of an old wooden boat beached on the sand and tasted of a mouldy apple from a storeroom. The white stained legs were like driftwood with the taste of salt in the air. I pulled open a stiff wooden drawer, inside were all the lighters he had ever used. I fingered them one by one recalling when it was his favourite. He loved his pipe and would always come down to his garage after his evening meal for a quiet smoke and rummage around. At Christmas and on his birthday it would be a special fat cigar to be savoured. Did I catch a faint whiff of that same smoke in the air? Was he watching me as I threw them away? I quietly slipped his remembered special lighter into my pocket to remind me."

There can, of course, also be bad memories that lurk in ones mind. Through meditation I have been able to make the choice that I don't want to hold onto them. I liken such things to a sticky black cobweb, how it clings and you can't get rid of it. But if you try hard enough you can. The same goes for bad memories, there is a choice either to have your mind cluttered up with them or not. They need to be singularly viewed in the light of day, worked through, faced and let go of. They are the minds way of keeping you trapped in the past, whereas with meditation the present is the place to be in. If you start to analyse what a memory is, it is just a collection of electrical impulses stored in your brain. Their danger lies in their ability to trigger the same emotional feelings that happened when the remembered event occurred. The choice appears simple, to choose to continue letting the memory operate the way it has always done or not.

Meditation has helped me to detach myself from my thoughts. I can now see that my mind and thoughts are not the real me. Yes, the thoughts I have are created by events I have experienced but experience is moulded by culture/society/social/peer/family groups. It is taking an objective stance when viewing our memories and not a subjective one. Meditation has taught me to step out of my own shoes and view them from a wider perspective. In fact I think it is more of throwing your shoes away altogether, take the risk and go barefoot. Your feet might get cut and bleed in the process but it will be a more pleasant way of walking altogether.

Meditation gives the knowledge, opportunity and means to clear the clutter from the mind. It appealed to me, as I was tired of my mind ruling my body and me as a person. I was always taken by joy I saw in spiritual teachers, it was a simple joy that bubbled up. There did not seem to be a cause of it, it did not depend on a particular event, it was just there. I could see it in others but I could not conjure it up within myself. My meditation teacher possessed it and through his teachings I began to understand that it couldn't be concocted within, it has to arise by itself. After I'd been meditating for a while, I started to get hints of it. When I enjoyed doing something, suddenly I became aware of the 'joy' within the enjoyment.

I looked back over my life and realised I had enjoyed many things yet what they lacked was the joy contained within. Joy is rather like a Russian doll, the ones that are inside each other and get smaller as you open each. Joy is deep within all those outer layers of enjoyment; it is there all the time. You might choose to just look at the large outer doll and be content with that or you can take the dolls apart one by one and go deeper until you find the smallest. There is real joy all along. If you go out looking for joy it will elude you but by remaining open to it, joy will find you.

When I realised that joy was missing in my life, I wondered how I had lost it. I could recall in my childhood that I was often joyful but not in my adult life. I was beginning to believe that it had totally disappeared from my life altogether. I would define joy as a good to be alive feeling that does not have a particular cause. So often enjoyment comes from a cause, it always depends on something to give rise to it be it a glass of wine, a good meal, a visit from a friend. Joy just is. A baby is joyful, full of life and so is a young child but over the years they become less so, until as an adult you wondered what it felt like.

As I write this on the computer an email comes through from an author, he's selling his book on how to write a book. As a diversion, I read one of his articles on how to get started he offered the advice of writing thank you card to the person who had helped you most that day and doing it for 30 days. You thanked them for how they had helped you and explained why. On the surface a short writing exercise but on a deeper level, when was the last time you were thanked, let alone received a card for it? Someone has to start the ball rolling, what better surprise gift than a thank you card. I thought to myself that is a joyful thing to do, a giving and sharing experience, a place to get started. Joy can be given to others as freely as the air we breathe, joy can be given in the gift of ones time.

We can all choose to let joy into our lives again but I feel it only starts to make a reappearance once some of the clutter is clearer from one's mind. Clearing away the debris to enable it to bubble up to the surface and express itself. Joy surrounds us all the time in nature, have you ever heard a bird's song that is not joyous? The dawn chorus is a cacophony of joy. Through practising meditation I have become more aware of birds song. I first noticed it when I was driving along in my car and heard a bird's song very clearly. The windows were closed and I was travelling at a normal speed yet a distinct birds song caught my attention. This has been my ongoing experience; it is as though the birds are showing me how joyful life can be. I am always struck by the clarity of song and that song is surrounded by silence. It is contained and held within the silence.

Death makes us realise just how precious and short our lives are.

If a person near to us is dying we want to prolong their life so that we can say or do all the things we wanted to do with them. Yet we are forced to let them go. Death is inevitable to each of us and something about which we cannot chose. I now see a person's death as their consciousness flowing back into the universal consciousness. It is a returning home to where they belong. My guru nearly died recently and the state he entered into he described as blissful and that is a wonderful welcome.

Chapter 8

Senses

I have noticed since I have been meditating that my senses have increased. I previously mentioned how I was able to hear bird song clearly through closed windows. My ears have become more finely tuned to detecting subtle noise, fingers brushing across my face, air entering my nostrils, the sound of a dress in the breeze. All sorts of noises that had previously gone unnoticed by me I try to capture creatively. I have quite a little game with myself in trying to capture the noise I hear in words. You could do it now, run your fingers through your hair and listen to the sound; mine sounds like the receding tide on a sandy beach.

As I have enjoyed silence more and more, I have chosen to eliminate unwanted noise from my life. I prefer to turn off the radio or television and have silence surrounding me. I find it so restful and therapeutic. To many people silence can seem threatening and it is preferable to have continual noise in order not to feel alienated. The point is missed, it does not alienate it connects you to something very special. Something that will enhance your life, it feeds your soul. Too often we shut off our senses in order not to feel overwhelmed but perversely we also pollute our senses with too much noise in order to numb them. Meditation leads you to silence and stillness yet both can equally be found in quietly sitting and allowing both to reveal themselves to you.

When actions are carried out in stillness and silence, they are enhanced and an awakening of all the senses can occur. It is the custom at the ashram to eat in silence in order to be aware of what is eaten. I can honestly say I have never tasted food better. Initially, when looking at my plate I am attracted by the different colours and textures of the food, then I can smell the various herbs and spices used. When I taste the food, each flavour can be savoured and I become aware of the different textures on my tongue. No water is taken whilst eating and the food is yogic, full of satva, meaning it is prepared with good thoughts and energy. Each meal eaten in this way can be a culinary delight. If you have been out to dinner with friends how often have you really tasted the meal you have eaten? Your mind being too busy in conversation. You can end up paying a fortune for it and get indigestion too boot. Each illustrates there is a lesson to be learnt by giving more attention to what we eat and the way we eat it. What a feast the first was, yet it was of simple food whereas the other might be a gourmet's delight but does not enhance ones health or life.

Another unusual by product of meditation is that your taste buds can become activated whilst meditating, in fact my mouth often waters. Not because I am thinking about food more to do with being in contact with the universal energies.

My sense of smell has also increased although sometimes I wish it hadn't. I can smell my neighbours pipe at a great distant carried on the wind, I can smell water, skin, all manner of things that I had not smelt before. It might not necessarily be good, as so often certain food smells overpower me and turn my stomach; particularly with meat. I do enjoy the aroma of flowers, hence my love of gardening but besides smelling flowers I appreciate touching their delicate petals; their feel deeply moves me.

Touch is the most beautiful sense we have, our fingertips are constructed to be wonderful receptors. Because I have had a skin problem, I marvel at other people's flawless skin that they take for granted. Healthy skin is only really appreciated when you don't have it any more, how often I have yearned for lump free skin. I have teasingly been called crocodile skin so you can guess what you would prefer to touch. I love a baby's skin, it is perfection but many a time I cast an envious gaze over just normal skin. Skin is lovely, warm and supple; great to touch and be touched. If you are cold you naturally run your hands up and down your arms to get heat. I have been teaching myself acupressure, reflexology, hand and head massage. It is all a way of respecting and loving yourself whilst using the sense of touch to its full advantage. Too often we are waiting for someone else to come along to do it for us and we can be in for a long wait, so do it to yourself.

One of the benefits of having a pet is its touch. I had my cat Daisy for seventeen years and each day of her life I stroked her, the feel of her soft, silky fur running across my hands, will never be forgotten. I was surprised when she died how much I missed her because she was never a friendly cat, too much hissing and sharp claws but she used to condescend to let me stroke her when she was in the mood or needed feeding.

Lastly to the sense of sight, along with the sense of stillness I have gained a sharper vision. It is as though everything that rests in stillness has the background of stillness to highlight it and make it stand out. Everything stands out in a sharper relief, the differentiation between the colours of the leaves on a tree, the detail of a greenfly or the wood grain of a table. It is like seeing with fresh eyes. The wonder is that it has been there all the time and I have seen it many times before but never really taken notice of it. I was mesmerised one day by a single raindrop hanging on a cobweb, the sunlight just caught it and reflected a spectrum of coloured light rays. The multicoloured rays burst forth like lasers, each containing the range of a painter palate, I was amazed and awe struck.

All our senses have been given to us to use but we only use a small proportion of them, I was one of the worst culprits for taking them for granted. It is only when they get taken away from us that we put a value on them and realise just how precious. Meditation was for me a wake up call to use my senses to their full. I have always been taken by colour and love wearing brightly coloured clothes but it was not until art classes that I gained a fuller understanding of how to create a colour. I first worked with watercolours but it took a lot of practice to be able to mix a colour. On an Open College course I learnt about warm and cool colours and how they should be used to their full effect. Painting taught me how to look, to look not just at shapes but colour and shade. Art is a sensory medium and it has brought me much pleasure. I have greatly appreciated my ability to stop and stare and really look at things in detail.

Chapter 9

Art

I had always envied people who could paint and I enjoyed looking at other artist's work. I assumed it was only for people who were naturally creative and not for me. Throughout the past ten years, I've had to challenge this assumption of my creative abilities, as well as encourage those who I encounter to do the same. I never imagined that by taking the first step of going to an art class that I would end up using art therapeutically. I like to encourage others to take that initial risk of trying something new and not letting negative thoughts stop you from doing it.

For what I can remember of art at school, was when I painted a very good impression of a daffodil and I was really pleased with it, hoping praise from the teacher. Her dismissive remarks heralded the end of any hope of mine to an artistic life, soon after I dropped art as a subject and replaced it with biology.

Throughout my life I always wished I could pick up a paintbrush and recreate the scene on canvas. Just the freedom of moving the paint around and doing something representational would have been good enough, just letting inner emotions express themselves on paper. But there was a big void between wishing to do it, actually picking up a paintbrush and starting. A small incidence, whilst I was at a yoga day, changed my perception of what art could be. It was a craft exercise whereby coloured waxes were melted with a hot iron onto paper. Without even trying, an attractive conglomeration of colours appeared making an artistic piece of work that I was proud of, I held onto those pieces and appreciated looking at them from time to time. They gave me hope that I could actually be creative artistically.

It was through counselling that I became aware of this need to express myself creatively and through the support of counselling I was able to find the courage to be able to go to a class. We negotiated the steps I would need to take to find the right class and not set myself up for a fall before I even started. Finding the right class, chatting to teacher before hand and even attending the first class to see if it was suitable, before making a commitment. I did all this but still walked hesitantly through the classroom door on that first day. I needn't have worried, there were many fellow students in the same boat concerned about their artistic worth. The teacher was cheerful and fun loving, this gave us the confidence to try and not listen to those negative thoughts. We all helped each other and praised each others work, not in the sense of a general 'ooohh that's a lovely' but praising the good bits we could see in the work produced. None of us were that gullible to think our first endeavours were masterpieces but you could see for yourself the parts that were good and acknowledge them. So our confidence was gradually pieced back together.

I always remember in a latter life drawing class, after an hour of trying to get a hip curve right, the teacher talked about the poetry of the curve and I was so pleased as that's what I was trying to capture. It didn't matter that the rest of the body had proportion problems but that curve was perfect. It was a moment of understanding between the perceiver and the artist that was spot on and one that stays with you, this is what painting was all about.

In my first art class we worked from the book, 'Drawing from the right side of the brain' which proved to yourself that you could actually be artistic without realising it. From there we learnt to handle watercolours with still life, in the summer we progressed to going painting outdoors. Painting outside had a wonderful feel to it, the way the light changed and altered was a continual exploration.

When my art teacher said she was doing a painting holiday in Greece I jumped at the chance of going with her. It seemed hard to believe that from never having painted before I was going on a painting holiday for two weeks. We were very fortunate to stay at a lovely old rambling house in a very unspoilt part of Greece. The flowers, the buildings, landscapes all just waiting to be painted. All in the wonderful summer sunshine, with the heat, smells and atmosphere begging to be captured on canvas. Still no 'masterpieces' but at the end of the two weeks we had a small exhibition of our work. We all felt we'd come a long way within a short space of time and were able to pride ourselves on our achievements.

This holiday also signalled a change for me internally, I had stepped out as a person in my own right, I had left behind the role of wife and mother. It was as though my narrow horizons had expanded. It was the first time I'd been away from my family in twenty years and I had to act and think independently. I could focus on what I wanted and not have to think of others needs first. With the safety net of family roles taken away, it was an opportunity for me to gain a clearer understanding of what I wanted from my own life. In the past I had felt fulfilled with my family roles but as the children got older and more independent, their need for me grew less, I was forced to turn the spotlight on myself for a change. When I asked myself 'what did I want out of life?' I didn't know the answer. I began to wonder who I was exactly, where had my vivacity and enthusiasm of youth gone? Too often I'd weighed myself down with self-criticism and negativity but there comes a point when you think 'why am I letting these affect me so?' even to the point of stopping what I wanted to do. Art was one area that I could take the risk and try something new not letting my self-criticism get in my way.

It's not necessarily other people who find fault with us, we are past masters at doing it to ourselves. Seeing these destructive patterns in operation and saying to oneself 'stop it' and not letting them form a block. Okay I will never be a fantastic artist but I enjoy painting, if you don't take the opportunity you will never find out what you are capable of. What is the worst that could happen, failure? The crime could be that you might never have tried in the first place. Test your potential, move out of your comfort zone and take a risk. If we don't try new things there can be no personal growth and we are given this life as an opportunity to grow. A simple step like joining an art class activated my potential. I went onto further classes and workshops. I laughed, I had fun, I shared an interest with many delightful people. This part of my life kept expanding in unexpected kinds of way, I was surprised at the knock on effect of that one decision.

The greatest gift I have been given from learning to paint, is the gift of seeing. It has taught me to really look at every object anew, to look in detail to see the shadow, the subtle change of tones, and to identify warm or cool colours. The rich texture of seeing unfolds itself to me, I now take time to stop and look at everyday things. By closely studying say a flower in this way, you develop an intimate relationship with it, the artist and object merge. You enter into timeless space when you paint and you lose all track of time. When you stare at minute detail, for example you can wonder at the sight of the small hairs on a ladybird's legs, that you had never observed before. In everyday life opportunities to look abound, sometimes when I am in the mood I study the colour pattern of leaves on a tree, this leads to my pondering on just how many leaves are on one tree and how many trees there are in a field. As this process happens I become in awe of nature, its magnitude, its wonderous forms. I marvel at creation and the universe, how blessed we are to be able to enjoy it.

My awareness slowly has expanded and it ties in with my meditation practice. I am more able to connect with my surroundings and feel in harmony with them. Yet at the same time am stunned by how awesomeness nature is. The oddest things can make a lasting impression. Every morning I look out across my grass and see hundreds of cobwebs filled with dew hanging on the blades of grass. I ponder, that each has been made by a small spider and that same spider has survived the lawnmower – such industry despite the hazards. This is only one species of insect that lives hidden in my lawn, I ponder at the multitude of existence under my feet when I tread on it. It is an opportunity to absorb the magnitude of nature. Perhaps this is an obtuse benefit of learning to paint but a moment as above, be it a small spider connected me to the wholeness of the universe. Many such opportunities are there for the taking in every day life.

A more down to earth benefit of learning to paint was when I failed the final tape on my counselling course, I had fresh eyes to look around and see what was available to me and person centred art therapy was able to catch my eye. I had experience with counselling but always felt another media of expression was needed instead of just talking. Having overcome my own barriers in learning to paint, I felt I would be able to relate to those with similar difficulties and encourage them to use it as a therapeutic and self-exploratory medium.

Chapter 10

Failure

Failure is a harsh teacher; nobody wants to fail especially me I found. I cannot say I have had any big failures in my life so when a big one came along it really hit home. It all evolved around the final exams for my counselling course. I sailed through the theoretical essays and greatly enjoyed the challenge they presented. I gained top marks for them and therefore thought I could use the same techniques when it came to presenting an oral tape of my work. How wrong I was.

In the final year of the counselling course you were expected to take on clients. Many of my fellow students had experience in counselling clients previously and were also involved with various agencies or groups. I had to look for a placement in which to gain experience, so the search began. I eventually found one with youth work, as I had previously worked as a voluntary youth worker in my village for ten years. A youth information shop was starting up and I was pleased to be able to have the opportunity to counsel young people who would benefit from it. It took awhile to get the shop refitted and decked out but I patiently waited for the pleasant counselling room to be completed. It was decided on which evenings I could use it and the daytime staff would book the young people in for me. Often it was the case of them not turning up or not returning; my counselling experience remained very limited.

I turned to bereavement counselling and completed their various courses before I commenced. I counselled the bereaved in their homes and found it rewarding to be of help. Sometimes attachment issues would arise and a very close relationship would develop, particularly as I counselled in people's homes. These and similar matters I would take to my supervisor where we would discuss the best way in which to deal with them. I was very fortunate to have an excellent supervisor who adhered to all the professional guidelines; my standards of practice were spot on. She could quickly pick up on any omissions or errors that occurred and they were corrected. I prided myself in giving a safe and secure environment in which a client could self explore. I also had a bereavement supervisor and when I asked if I could record clients for my final tape, she checked and came back with the answer no. Reluctantly I had to look for another placement.

Searching for another placement proved difficult but I always tried to build on what experience I already had. Way back when I had left home and moved area, feeling homesick and lonely I looked for voluntary work to feel more integrated in the community. I decided to help out at a social group for the physically and mentally disabled as well as abled bodied people. Its aim was to encourage the breaking down of barriers between those with a disability and those not, in a friendly and fun atmosphere. Miscellaneous social activities and events were arranged and the experience of it greatly stayed with me. I was humbled by the way their disability was overcome and life lived, it also highlighted my own area of prejudice, often when I thought I had none. At one time I was at a game of five-aside basketball and they needed any extra person in a wheel chair. I could not bring myself to get into it. I could dance with people in wheelchairs but not get into one myself. It was as though I was frightened to see the world from a completely different perspective and could not bring myself to do it. I helped out for a couple of years but I never sat in a wheelchair. Disability came in many guises especially with the effects of thalidomide, small hands and feet protruding from a body. Yet when you saw the person on a dance floor enjoying themselves, it put it all into perspective, they were a person coping with a disability.

Later on when I was studying with the Open University I chose to study the handicapped in the community. Handicapped implying that it is the social environment that handicaps the person not the disability. It was a vast issue in itself and I visited homes, day centres and hospitals to gain a greater insight of what disability meant to a person.

All the same time I had to tackle the unknown prejudices that I never expected I had. It was before the old mental homes were disbanded and we had arranged to visit one. We arrived early and peeped through the window. What I saw greatly disheartened me; a crowd of people were aimlessly walking around making funny noises. I was filled with dread at having to go in there and wondered about my safety and the safety of my young daughter I had with me. A short time later when we entered, it was a completely different atmosphere, that same crowd greeted us with interest and warmth. It had been their dinner break and they had not known how to occupy their time hence the wandering and the blank looks. They were entranced with my young daughter and continually wanted to touch her. I realised how little contact they had with the outside world yet they still wanted to maintain human contact. Often being institutionalised and contained by four walls it seemed insurmountable to them that there was a different life outside but these same poor souls were put out to care in the community to fend for themselves a short while later, when the government disbanded mental hospitals.

A lot changed in the next twenty years whereby disability became more acceptable and visible. The environment slowly changed to make it more user friendly for them. They were living in the community on their own and these were the next people I chose to counsel. I still had not knocked all my prejudices on their head, when sexual intercourse came on the agenda I had assumed it could not happen because of the presenting physically disabilities but these were just ordinary young people with ordinary desires. I counselled them in their homes and gained a close knowledge of their problems but I felt it inappropriate to record my sessions with them for the final exam. I also wished to widen my counselling experience and sought another venue.

A fellow student was doing very well at a GPs practice nearby, she had got the GPs to take her on and introduce counselling into the surgery. This was no mean achievement at the time because up to then doctors were very anti counselling. It was only a new up and coming treatment, not tried and tested, doctors still had their reservations about it. They had to be convinced that counselling worked and the proof of the pudding is in the eating, as they say. She worked wonders and gave a very professional service and was soon recruiting fellow students to join her. I approached her and was warmed by her response that she believed I was a good counsellor and could join her team.

The doctors referred the patients to us and we would start with a minimum contract of six weekly visits, we had to hold our sessions in a consulting room after surgery hours, which was not an ideal environment. I was thrown in at the deep end; depression, failed suicide, dying; heavy issues came in abundance. I kept my boundaries firm and professional and was very client centred. It was a success and the doctors gradually began to realise the value of counselling.

I was still very reluctant to ask clients if I could record them, I felt it to be an invasion of their privacy but I had to produce a tape. Sometimes they were happy for me to record as practice but I often found my voice was very difficult to hear.

A fellow student offered herself to be counselled for my first tape and I felt okay with that but apprehensive. I had unresolved issues about being judged and I felt the tape was a way of judging me. My colleague felt the benefit of the session and thought me to be a good counsellor. I analysed the tape to the best of my ability and hoped it would pass, it did not. It was a blow which took the wind out of me. I was disheartened but several others had failed too, with whom I could commiserate and at the back of my mind I knew I had another opportunity with a different tape. It was hard to accept failing when the majority had passed and there was also the question of some people who I felt should not have passed. I could not understand how they had managed to pass and I had not.

The next time I approached a friend who was doing the same course but at a different college and understood the rules of the game. She had a particular issue she wanted to look at and that is just what we did. I was most apprehensive about doing the tape, as with each try the chances of gaining my diploma diminished. It was as though the goal post got further moved away. That by failing first time I have highlighted my inadequacies and they would be sought out next time to prove that they were right the first time. I got the false bravado, I will show you this time, you will see just how good a counsellor I am but living up to my verbal encouragement was harder to do than I expected.

It was with trepidation that I went to get the result of my second tape. It was a Friday afternoon that I went to see my tutor and to receive that penetrating blow to my stomach. The invigilator had checked the tape so there was not doubt I had failed again. I was given the offer of repeating the last term in order to improve my chances of passing. I walked back to my group with a very heavy heart. I had to stand up in front of them all with my failure clearly on display. As I saw their concerned faces all I could do was burst out crying and sob out the outcome. Their kind words of encouragement and belief in me did not seem to touch me, I felt humiliated, I had let myself down. That scene was etched on my memory, that I can still see it today and remember those same feelings.

I did not feel able or want to repeat the last term especially as it would be with a new group of people. I felt cared for by the group I was in and that had been built up over two years of trust, I could not leapfrog into unknown territory and show all my vulnerabilities to strangers all over again. I chose just to get on with it and try again. My tutor offered his help in processing my tape but my pride stood in my way. We had an uneasy relationship over the two years on the course, he believed in using gestalt techniques to make people change. I felt these were too forceful if you were in a vulnerable state. We never saw eye to eye on many things but I did respect him as a tutor. We were meant to be the two sides of a coin and I was never able to avoid his personal development group even when names were picked out of the hat, as much as I would have liked to. There was only one moment that we became as one when we acknowledged our shared skin complaints. I think it was that we were both too similar and disliked in the other what we disliked in ourselves, so I was not inclined to accept his offer of help.

I started to record the client I was most working with. After finishing at the doctors surgery he came with me to be counselled privately. He was a failed attempted suicide and our work was on going, amounting to two years. Yet again my voice was always too soft on the tape and could only just be heard but persevere I did and produced a transcript of one. I analysed it and sent it off to the tutor's home address.

As I write those last two sentences I realise I have replayed my avoidance technique of hiding pain, I have skipped over all the pain that went on at that time. Failing actually knocked me for six; I thought if I just kept trying I would get there in the end. It was my 'try hard' driver that I had always run on and now it was not working, I was at a loss. No matter how hard I tried I could not do it. The likelihood of passing was getting less and less. My whole self-esteem was based on trying hard, with determination and patience I thought I would get there, but this was not working either. My worth was set on getting qualified, with a piece of paper saying I was qualified I could be a counsellor, without that I was not one. I felt utterly worthless, it did not matter that I had completed the two years and passed everything except this tape. It was all wiped out by failure. Other feelings of my worthlessness crept in; if I did not pass I must be useless at relating to people. I cannot tell you the depths of despair I plunged into but I kept these to myself. Needless to say all that repression has to take a physical form and I developed a stomach ulcer. The pain from it was minor compared to the devastation to my self-esteem. Each day that ulcer burnt into my stomach and each day my self-esteem got lower. I could easy find more ammunition to stoke its fires. But there got to a point when I could not sink any lower I had run out of ways to chastise myself.

It was then that I became aware of what I was doing to myself. All my life I had hung my self-esteem on things from outside. It had relied on other people or influences to be strong. If I gained admiration it increased it, criticisms diminished it. It could fluctuate that easily from day to day. My self worth depended on others' view of me not how I viewed myself. I had to learn to value myself. All the roles I had performed in my life had covered how I really felt about myself. By pleasing others I had always got positive responses, which was great for my ego. I could say to myself what a good caring person I am, look at what all these people think of me. At no time did I want to look at what I thought of myself. It was the wake up call I needed. None of it happened over night, my stomach ulcer lasted for months. Looking back it was something that needed to happen if my own self worth was to be developed.

I can remember on the final day of the course going up to the tutor and saying that perhaps I would thank him one day for it. I do not know why I said it, it just came out and at the time I was highly unlikely to ever thank him.

In the work I have done since I have had reason to give thanks especially with meditation the ego is a very useless tool to have, it just obstruct one's progress at every turn. Since my ego had such a big knock by failure it has been easier to eliminate it for meditation. I had sampled the black whole of nothingness and it was okay.

All this was going on whilst I was trying to complete my tape and I felt a wave of relief as I got it into the post. Unbeknown to me I had taken down the tutor's address wrongly. When I found out I was fraught, I could not possibly put myself through that again. When I found out my error I got onto the post office to try and chase it. I found out there was a slight difference between a flat and his house. I wrote to the flat in desperation, no reply. Eventually as I would not stop crying my husband went to the flat to collect it and take it to the tutor, explaining how I had missed the cut off date and how upset I was. I need not have worried myself as it was all a waste of time and I failed that tape too.

By that point in time the worst was over, I could not have felt any more demolished than I had done. It was now a time for rebuilding. When I eventually got my certificate through saying I had completed the hours and theoretical requirements but not passed the diploma, I could pride myself on what I had achieved. There was still the issue of telling people about it, there always remained the element of shame at failure but tell people I had to. I have to remind myself what I have learnt from the process of failure, what inner resources I have had to draw on, how I came through it and out the other side. I learnt to deal with failure and can now keep it in perspective. It will not wipe me out as a person as it did before. I have built up my self worth from nothing. I cannot say I liked not gaining the diploma but it does not mean I am a bad counsellor. I give thanks to all those friends, colleagues, supervisors and counsellors who saw me through it. They saw the real me, the vulnerable me, the frightened me and they accepted me just the way I was. We learn our biggest lessons from failure and it can provide the fertilizer for personal growth.

Chapter 11

Ego

We all think our ego is so necessary to us as a person, that without it we are nothing. But in reality it is nothing but a hindrance to our development and personal growth. The experience of the biggest failure I had in my life taught me that.

In meditation the aim is to blend with the oneness that exists, that there is no separation between you and consciousness, you are both part of the wholeness. Do you think your ego wants to blend in? No it does not. It wants to stick with its own self-importance. It wants to stay at the top of the heap exclaiming that it's here and wants to be listened to. It only has its self-perpetuation at heart and I would also question if it has a heart at all.

I agree with Freud's view of the ego, which is separate from the id and superego. Id being 'instinctual urges' and the superego being society's influences. The ego is the individual part of ourselves which balances the two but it is still not the person. The ego is full of its own self importance, it has to remain in charge for its survival. I am slowly turning to the belief that the individual person is an expression of the universal consciousness that exists. I come by this through experience and gradually realising that it is so. I have gone by the premise that I would not believe what I was taught or what I read in a book, I would wait till I actually experienced it for myself, then I would know it to be true. You might site this is imagination or wishful thinking but meditation creates a wakeful state where what is seen is clear. When the same experiences are repeated I started to know there was more to it. I am sceptical by nature and like proof, I am not given to trance like states, my feet are firmly on the ground. Yet through meditation I can enter expanding spaces that are very peaceful. Some people experience great joy but what I appreciate from the experiences I have is that they are free from feelings and emotions. It is freedom, freedom from everything.

When I have been in that inner state of freedom, I realise the oneness of everything. There is no separation, it is all part of the whole. Unity has a wonderful aura but it does not need the ego to get in its way. The ego takes on the battle with unity, it will try to obstruct and hinder your spiritual progress. The ego wants to keep its self-importance. It was always a puzzle to me how each person on this planet could be filled with their own self-importance that they are the centre of their own world and everything in it revolves around them. All these egos believing to some degree or another that they were top dog. I don't mean this in a detrimental way, it is just the way we view our world. How could it be that each individual life was so special? It was a conundrum I had struggled with all my life. Billions of egos fighting for supremacy, no wonder we fight wars. Of course nothing is as simple as that but we need to personally review our ego to see how they operate for us. What are the good bits and what are the bad? What functions well and what does not? To be able to differentiate between the two. You might be quite happy the way you are but if you wish to progress on a spiritual path it will need to be revised.

The experience of failure gave me the opportunity of taking a long hard look at my ego and to assess how useful it was to me. This has developed further when I was first starting to practice meditation. The ego runs the mind with its incessant chatter, when you try to shut the chatter off, you realise you have a fight on your hands. Your mind and ego do not want to be closed down. The ancient text of the Bhagavad Gita explains the same problems in dramatic symbolic story form in the battles of Arjuna, which is still used today for spiritual guidance.

If only it were that easy to drop one's ego in order to meditate, sometimes it is easier to put it onto one side at first and pick it up afterwards. Change is a subtle thing that can creep up on you unawares but you have to start with the intention first. Little by little I am reducing the strength my ego has over my life. I can see when it arises, acknowledge what is happening but not let it influence what I am doing. The answer is not giving fuel to its fires by attending to it instead saying 'okay I can see you', patting it on its head and leaving it at that, getting on with what I am doing.

I sometimes view the ego like a coat, I put it on to go outside and face the world but I do not need it on internally when I meditate. I appreciate losing myself in the oneness that exists. When I meditate there is no me, I cannot be found, I am limitless. I have expanded into the oneness of existence – that is freedom. I am becoming to understand the teaching of Advaita, non-dualism. There is no it and I; both are part of the wholeness. Initially I had a job getting my thinking around the concept of non-dualism but by practicing meditation it has revealed itself to me. My mind could not quite grasp it, I thought I knew when I didn't but by actually experiencing I know what it is.

I always feel that the ego is rather like a gremlin sitting on my shoulder. It rarely says anything good about me, and just gets on with continually criticising all that I do. I will not be good enough, I will never make the grade, I will make a fool of myself. The list is endless in its content and variety. But there came a point when I said enough is enough, I do not need this self criticism I can do without it, where is the off button? Meditation techniques I learnt later provided that off switch.

It is all about realising your self worth, not giving yourself a hard time. Being compassionate and loving towards your self. Forgiving yourself for past misdemeanours and letting them go, do not continually relive them or beat your self up with guilt. So often we are shackled by the past, which hinders our personal growth. It is good to come to a realisation of this then the choice arises either to stay in that pattern of behaviour or change it. Although change is not easy it is possible to achieve with perseverance then the many benefits can be reaped. No longer will you be troubled by the same things, they will be eradicated for good. Meditation can avoid hours of psychoanalysis, it allows you to view your life objectively seeing the way the mind works and not be drawn into its games.

Meditation gives the opportunity to move from the small self, the limited ego, into experiencing the bigger Self. The universal consciousness that exists, which encompasses everything within its embrace. What a journey to make from learning about the ego initially on the counselling course to actually finding a way to dissolve its hold on one's personality through meditation. Swami Ramana Maharshi, a great spiritual teacher suggested posing the question to oneself 'Who am I?' continually, in order to discover who one is under the covering of personality. So with my spiritual search, I have questioned 'who am I?' and thus I started to look into the many corners of my life.

Chapter 12

Closeness

It is hard to describe the dividing line when closeness turns to 'don't be close' and vice versa. When on the counselling course studying transactional analysis I was able to look at this more closely. That we are driven by the drivers we adopt unconsciously. One of mine was 'don't be close'. This is a message that you carry inside your subconscious outwardly I was friendly and enjoyed peoples company. I was naturally close to those near to me but it was more a question of expressing it to those new outside my family circle. I was never brought up to be a hugging and kissing type of person. Most of my friends were brought up the same way, so it caused me no problems. That was until I went on the counselling course, the requisite being you regularly hugged people to comfort them in their pain. Remembering one's own painful memories and share them, which would involved more hugging and lots of tears, either yours or theirs. If I had been told this would be the case before I joined, I would never have gone. It was what my worst nightmares were made of and I had two years of it. If anyone tells me they are thinking of doing a counselling course, I question if they know what they're letting themselves in for because I certainly didn't. In retrospect it was something I had to confront but did not want to and I was fortunate to be given that safe environment for change to happen.

It didn't occur overnight but slowly over the two years, I could allow my feelings to naturally surface and express themselves. I always found it easier to comfort others and put my arms around them, whilst they cried. It was a strange feeling when I was emotionally upset to have others put their arms around me and for me to allow it. Even a sympathetic look could open up the floodgate of tears but I could cry without embarrassment. As a child and as an adult it was an unspoken rule never to cry in public, tears were to be hidden away from sight. When I was upset, tears would be shed alone in my room. By the next morning, I would put back on my bright face and go out to meet the world; no one being any the wiser. Through the counselling course I was able to let others see my tears, it was a testing ground for doing it safely before doing it in the big wide world. In this giving and sharing atmosphere I felt accepted and loved and have tried to be more extrovert in expressing my emotions ever since. By counselling others, I hoped to provide them with a safe environment to look at their own fears and concerns, as well as giving space for a natural expression of their emotions and feelings.

Through counselling I challenged my 'don't be close' driver, I tested out new ways of behaving in the counselling course group setting and found them to be safe and nurturing. I slowly became aware of my unmet needs and realised I was not caring for myself. It was because of these earlier experiences I was able to express my feelings about being unlovable to a group in Greece. It has been a long process of learning to love myself, the good bits and well as the bad bits. To be compassionate and patient with myself. Accepting I no longer have to be perfect, I can have faults and I can still remain lovable.

I have had to readjust how I view myself, to see myself worthy of consideration. I found if I viewed myself as a separate person I could add myself into the equation. In amongst considering family and friends I included myself in it. I was determined to give this new person (called me) some of my time just as I did to the others. It might seem a perverse way of viewing things but it worked. It enabled me to give myself some much needed time to do what I wanted to. It was rather like another person taking care of me, when I felt tired it would say 'its okay to sit down put your feet up, read a magazine, eat chocolate biscuits'. This is just a simple example, needs can be big or small but it helped me to adopt a nurturing attitude towards myself, and not go on over looking myself. I recognised I did have needs that I could meet, I had a right to freely express them in an appropriate manner and they did not necessarily have to be at the cost of others. If I have an important need, I should take note of it and see how it can be met. Not just operate as I did in the past and hope it would be met by someone else. How often had I expected my husband to be a mind reader, see my need and meet it. Now I'm not prepared to always put my own needs last, as I previously did. This has become easier to do as my children have grown up and their needs have lessened, which has lightened the load. Yet how easy it is to refill your life with other people's needs to make yourself feel valued and one has to be aware of the processes involved. Where does one's self-esteem lie in that, if one's self-esteem is thin like rice paper it can be easily torn.

My guru's main work has been teaching me to love myself, slowly over time this is coming to fruition. I can now give myself huge imaginary hugs, the warmth of that love seeping through to my bones. I can love my faults. My fiery short temper, swearing, drinking; these can all be viewed in a compassionate light. I am human, I have human weaknesses. I would like to eliminate my faults but they are just as much a part of me as the good ones. I can even admire and acknowledge my good points, without becoming vain or self obsessed. I love me for being me and that makes me happy. I can be frustrated annoyed, happy or miserable, they are all different aspects of me as a person. They do not make me a bad person or a good one, it's just the way I am. Other people can knock me but that is not going to change how I feel about myself and that is the greatest benefit of it all. Your self worth is not dependant on others and that for me has been a long journey in itself.

On the counselling course we were encouraged to physically express ourselves through touch. This was quite early on in the course and wasn't something I looked forward to. I thought to myself I could act this out, doing what was expected of me but it wasn't that easy. Some of my female companions were totally at ease with touching and stroking another woman; how I did not run for the hills I will never know. I braved it out and as it was done in a non-threatening manner with genuine care for me, I was able to relax and let myself go to what the moment would bring. I was surprised it was a pleasurable feeling that arose not embarrassment and I could let myself be touched and hugged. In turn I could touch and hold my fellow partners and feel warmth from it.

I was very fortunate to have a lovely large lady who was especially good at hugging. They were like big bear hugs, all cosy and soft. I can remember their feel to this day and she taught me a lot. The relationships she had had in her life were not particularly good ones and she remained single, but boy could she hug. What a loss to her possible partners. Women out numbered the men on our course and there were several sensitive men on it. One in particular who had a rough ride through life and was overcoming it, he gave equally memorable hugs. I marvelled at his ability to overcome childhood abuse and still give the most wonderful hugs. These two special people never knew how much they helped me, I never spoke to them about it at the time. It has been easier in retrospect to say when I have seen the ripples of its effects in my life. As I got braver and when the need arose I was able to approach these giving souls and ask for hugs. I just loved being hugged by them. It was a nurturing feeling to be given a hug that contained no hidden agenda; it was just given out of love. Too often love is linked to sexual love and is trapped in its narrow confines. It cuts us off from being able to embrace a fellow being just because they are there and for no other reason. When I was bringing up my children, I made sure I gave them plenty of hugs; yet they both have grown up with the same reticence that I had. It makes one question if these things are handed down in the genes and it takes a special effort to overcome them.

Although attitudes towards displays of affection are more acceptable nowadays and I can see the changes that have occurred since I was a child. We still are behind in feeling as at ease with it as other cultures are. Maybe because I am older it is more expected that kissing and hugging friends and relatives are part of the meeting and leaving ritual. Through the learning experience on the counselling course I came to realise the importance of embracing another person and in my counselling practice I was always prepared to give a hug if needed. I always made the point of checking to see if that was what the person really wanted. I remembered my feelings whereby I felt threatened at the intimacy of a hug and that they might feel the way I had previous done. Often there was no need to ask, in emotional situations of self-exploration their eyes sought mine for comfort and you knew they were feeling as vulnerable as a small child in need of reassurance. A hug was beyond words.

As part of the counselling course you were expected to have received counselling yourself to enhance your own self-awareness and this was where my greatest failing lay. I wrongly assumed having studied psychology and sociology for my Open University degreee, that I knew all the answers and could easily analyse myself in this manner. I could see how I'd been moulded into set behaviour patterns, I could self analyse with a clinical precision that won me great marks in essays. Freud was a favourite where I could identify with his libidinal energies yet somehow in it all, I missed out the me. I was not the object of the exercise I was the subject. Through eventually having counselling towards the end of the course, I found out just how painful it was to be the subject. To sit and go through very difficult memories and past events, to let the bottled up emotions and feelings arise, takes a lot of courage. I gained a great respect for those that I counselled in the future.

Being a client myself enabled me to identify out-of-date behaviour patterns I was running my life on, giving me the opportunity to change them. I now realise change is an easy word to say but very difficult to make happen. You have to want it to make it happen, very badly in fact otherwise it will not work. Too often you hope that someone else will make the change occur for you, in particular the counsellor themselves. Then the realisation comes it's only you that can do it nobody else. Problems are like balls of tangled string that take a lot of untangling, by slowly pulling out one strand at a time it can be untangled and you are left with a reusable piece of string, still as strong and undamaged. Counselling is finding the same within you, you can learn much from the process and emerge a wiser and more compassionate person. Compassion for yourself and for others, is another wonderful gift to be given. With the right counsellor who provides a nurturing environment you can feel the unconditional love that genuinely exists between all human beings, but has been covered up by multiple layers of socialisation.

Self-exploration in a one to one counselling situation is hard enough, doing the same but in a group situation is a very different kettle of fish. Every Friday afternoon on the counselling course was my dread. It was our time for the 'personal development group', whereby fifteen of us sat in a circle to explore our personal issues. I can honestly say I loathed sitting there, I have never felt at ease in large group, let alone bringing to light problems I had in front of others. I could discuss them on a one to one basis but if there was more than one person, I would feel very exposed. It was as though, if I gained two opinions on a personal issue, it would be too much for me to take in. I was not able to voluntarily speak out in the group; words would not form and I could not find a voice to speak with. Instead of its purpose of opening people out, it made me shrink more within myself, as though I was protecting something very precious within me. If pushed I could talk about issues that arose within the group but I could not fully partake. I found the whole situation a means of torture that had to be endured. I knew others felt the same as we discussed it but the majority were able to make good use of it. It takes a lot of experience in this type of groups to reap their benefits. We were able to support each other at difficult times of self-exploration and this I felt to be its main benefit. It has taken many years of working in groups to overcome my difficulties, now when I work with groups myself I can empathise with those that find similar difficulties.

Meditation has greatly helped me in being less self conscious in group situations and has enabled me to drop my ego, to get on with the doing and leave the me out of it. To just be fully there in the present. It is the 'me' part of me who feels uncomfortable in groups so if I leave the me out of it, the actual doing has become a lot easier. Shyness and embarrassment are all attached to my ego for a variety of reasons. They were old patterns of behaviour, which were outdated and inappropriate and equally had to be resolved.

It was because of these experiences I was later able in a meditation group to express myself openly and show my tears, without fear of repercussion. When a larger issue arose of thinking myself unlovable, I was able to tackle it.

Chapter 13

Lovability

It came as quite a shock to me to realise that I thought myself unlovable. It happened when I was out in Greece on a two week intensive yoga holiday. I had gone out to Greece in the summer of 2001. After being a wife and mother for so long, I tended to forget that I was a person who could function in their own right. In everyday life you have the safety net of the familiar around you, familiar people and places. It took courage to step outside that security and move into the unknown, to go it alone.

I had always enjoyed yoga and felt I could benefit from an intensive two week course. Playing on the safe side I opted to stay in the nearby hotel as opposed to staying at the centre which would have involved sharing a small room and washing facilities. I was not ready yet to give up my creature comforts that easily. Not being in the centre meant I had to make more of an effort to be involved and not keep myself separate. We were a very mixed crowd with very different tastes and temperaments but over meals and in spare moments it was enjoyable to get to know my companions personally.

The course involved a lot of Iyengar and Astanga yoga, which was quite strenuous for me as I have been used to Hatha yoga but I was willing to give it my best shot. We were also offered an additional meditation course taught by a young monk, which I decided to partake in. One day when I was in the small group learning a new meditation technique which involved repeating an affirmation that you love yourself, I found I was not able to do it, then it suddenly struck me I thought myself unlovable. The facilitator provided a warm and caring environment where I was able to say what I felt in front of the whole group. As I did so the tears started to course down my cheeks, unstoppable hot burning tears. I looked through the haze of tears at the teacher and there was an instant unsaid recognition between us that he knew just how it felt. After the group dispersed and I sat alone with him, we were able to sit in silence together while the tears continued to flow. Our eyes met and he shared my pain, our souls touched.

As we gathered for our evening meal, other members of the groups slowly gathered around me. Initially one woman said how brave she thought me to express myself so openly; she then went on to explain she was bulimic and also had felt herself unlovable. Another spoke of the hatred she felt against her mother plus a rape attack she'd endured. We naturally formed a support group for each other, and were able to openly express our deepest feelings without fear of repercussions. Others joined us, what became evident was that there was a general consensus that we all felt ourselves unlovable to one degree or another. Often it's buried so deep that it never rises to the surface to be reviewed, and as with me I'd developed many different coping strategies to keep it well at bay.

If you had met me then you might have seen a balanced woman managing quite well in life. I was optimistic, always made the best of any opportunities life dealt me. I was naturally cheerful, liked to laugh and had a sense of fun. I was surrounded by plenty of family and friends, I was a 'people pleaser' and this greatly helped. In Transactional Analysis terms I ran on two drivers to' please others' and 'try hard'. The end result being I was popular and well liked. The strategy I used worked and therefore I continued to run with it unhindered. The underlying script I used was 'don't be close' and 'don't feel', which might seem contradictory at first glance.

An exasperated tutor on a counselling course I was on, snapped one day and said 'don't you feel anything?' I gave him a shocked look, as he clearly did not understand, it was not a case of not feeling, 'it was a case of feeling too much' which had created my shut down. In retrospect it was when I was a young child I was overwhelmed by too many demands for attention from adults. The only way I could cope was to shut off my feelings and just act out what people wanted from me. A smiling interested face, a polite and friendly manner, a cheerful disposition; the list can go on. Somehow in amongst all this I'd lost my true identity. Even as an adult I was unaware of my own needs. Yes I was great at meeting other people's needs but no one ever asked me what mine were and I never even asked myself it. It was as though my needs came at the bottom of the pile and I was too busy fulfilling others to find that space to do so. Of course this was one area I had no intention of ever really tackling until the moment I was confronted head on, no holes barred with the stark fact that I really did think myself unlovable. Then the hard work began of unravelling the tangled ball of my past, which had brought me to this sudden revelation.

It's amazing that on one level, I functioned very well in life. I loved my husband and children and they loved me back. If others loved me, I didn't need to love myself. I always got my need for love met by others. If I couldn't get people to love me, I'd get them to admire me. I was described as attractive when I was a teenager and I always came out well in photographs therefore it was a natural progression to choose modelling as a career. I dressed well, enjoying the latest fashions in the late 60's and early 70's. It was a fun time to be in where fashions changed every week and I was keen to follow the most outrageous trends. Hence I got myself noticed and admired at the same time, what more could I want? Of course life is not so kind, especially in the modelling world and there were putdowns. I dealt with them as best I could but stopped modelling and just got on with my life, taking a secretarial course and changing direction. But that didn't stop me fully partaking in the fashions of the moment and having fun with it. With a sense of humour I could wear a paisley silver cat suit, a fur coat and a green straw hat all at once. I admired my grandmother's nonchalance when I accompanied her on a visit to a formal garden and I caused many a head to turn and stare. But attention or admiration is no substitute for loving yourself. Loving yourself enough to make sure your needs get taken care of, that you leave something for yourself and not always give it out to others.

I was surprised and shocked that I had covered my belief I was unlovable so well. To hit it head on like that was quite a blow. A benefit of meditation is that it allows deep rooted unconscious negative behaviour patterns to surface in a gentle way, to be dealt with, accepted that it had happened and for it to be let go of. Never to bother you again. You do not have to psychoanalyse it or trace it back, as I have done. Just let what needs to surface, surface and then let it go. Meditation is a clearing process that can allow all the blocks we put on ourselves to clear and they clear in the safe space of meditation. You do not feel overwhelmed or out of control and it is okay to cry, to let the sadness out. So often in similar group settings I would have hidden my feelings but in the safe environment provided I was able to reveal them, to be able to share them with others and for them to do the same. It was a deeply touching experience that I carried home with me.

Whilst on the course in Greece I was initiated by the same monk into the techniques he taught, it was a very beautiful and moving ceremony. I was struck by the conviction and dedication of my teacher, it was a very special moment in time. I returned home to practise. I was just eager to progress further on my path. Shortly after I started tai chi classes and slowly with my meditation and yoga practice I began to gain a clearer understanding of what was being accessed by all three – universal energy.

Chapter 14

Energy

What scientific proof is there to show that there really is a spiritual aspect to ourselves? My answer to this would be energy, spiritual energy in fact. Everyone accepts the reality of electricity; it is a modern fact of our everyday world. We cannot actually see it but we know it makes things work. If you put your fingers in a plug socket you would get a nasty shock but in a reduced form it can heat a fire element that you can warm your hands against. These are indisputable facts and we can understand the creation of electricity. When we look towards spiritual energy it is hard to comprehend its source and is the object of much conjecture, but leaving that aside for the moment I would like you to take on board that a spiritual energy does exist. It is as though there is a big generator in the universe and humans are the small capacitors that receive it.

Spiritual energy is called chi in Chinese and prana in India, it is a life force that descends from the universe (called universal energies or cosmic force), through into our solar system. As it passes through our solar system some of it is changed into solar energy. It is well known that the sun can produce vitamin D in our skins, which in turn helps our immune system. As the universal energies descend further they are absorbed by our planet Earth into the food we eat, the air we breathe, into the very ground itself which feeds our trees and plants. They in turn also absorb this universal energy, as does every living thing on this planet. But all this goes on unseen and you might wonder where the proof of all this is.

How does the average human begin to know about these energies? My answer would be, by experiencing them for yourself. Meditation and yoga first introduced me to these energies and it started a journey self-exploration to understand them.

It all began when I went on a two-week yoga holiday to Greece, it was my first time of intensive practice of yoga. It included Hatha, Iyenga and Astanga yoga, I found it quite strenuous to keep up the practice, as others were more advanced then me but I worked at my own pace. Towards the end of the two weeks, when I sat in the meditation posture of crossed legs on the floor, there seemed to be a vortex of energy ascending up from my base chakra to the top of my spine. This created a twirling feeling whereby my whole body joined in. Nobody offered me an explanation of it. I assumed that when I returned home it would stop but it did not and continued to differing degrees each time I sat down to meditate.

I was at a loss what to do about it, so I just accepted what was happening and got on with meditating. Eventually the twirling would calm down and centre itself in my spine. It was when I first went out to Spain for Energy Enhancement that I gained an understanding of what was occurring. The first initiation into energy enhancement meditation is aligning the spine with the universal energies. With the swami's help I was able to align my spine at right angles to the earth, which allowed the universal energies to flow down it. The twirling stopped instantly and has never returned. The spine can be seen as an aerial for the universal energies, operating in a similar way to a television aerial whereby signals can be received. We are all aerials for this spiritual energy and it is naturally flowing into and out of us all the time, but we are normally unaware of what is happening. It was much later that I read books on Kundalini energy and the chakras that I gained a deeper understanding.

From this same course I was able to work with the concept of earth energies grounding you to the planet and ascending up the spine from the base chakra. It opened up a whole new field of study. The energy enhancement course involves working with both universal and earth energies in a variety of meditations. Initiations are given into each and then it is up to oneself to practice them regularly.

At the same time of doing the course I was given the opportunity to receive reiki one initiations. I had never experienced reiki before and did not know what to expect but from the moment the swami laid her hands on my head for the first time, I knew what spiritual energy was. I soared up with the angels; I was deeply moved and elevated at the same time. I could feel the energies entering my body, I realised this was not imagination but true experience as I sat in a relaxed state. Every time I received an initiation I ended up crying, tears of elevation and tears that melted past emotions away. After each I felt deeply moved, calm, solid and fully present.

It was through the reiki and energy enhancement meditations that I came to know more about spiritual energies. Their forms could be varied but it was always from the same source. The energies were just a signpost to what was beyond them. They were just the surface expression of something greater. Just like waves on the ocean beneath them are the unfathomable depths of the ocean itself. I could list a multitude of sensations I felt, yet they are personal to each individual person, the point being is that they are real and they work, just like electricity they can be felt.

After the energy enhancement courses I returned home to practice and weaved the energies alongside my normal practice of meditation in stillness and silence. It was during this time that I joined a local tai chi class to learn the short form. We did a lot of warm up exercises to increase the chi in our bodies and after time I could feel a magnetic ball of energy between my hands, as the energy increased so did the size of the ball. It was the first time I felt this energy contact between my palms and over the years this has developed. It was a gradual deepening of my understanding of tai chi , what the energies did and were used for. I particularly liked the standing meditations as in chi gong, which involved channelling universal and earth energies through my body.

It has been a slow and gradual process of learning to work with the energies and after each tai chi class I always feel energised and well. You can read about these concepts in books but they will mean nothing unless they are practised regularly. They do not increase by themselves you have to first be open to them and allow them to work through you. It is a conscious effort of letting go and not trying to achieve anything. Not setting yourself up to be the best pupil. It is quite amusing in the class that there seems an epidemic of forgetfulness and each of us in turn forgets different parts of the form but that does not detract from its effectiveness or enjoyment.

I remained quite happy practising yoga and meditation daily on my own and attending a weekly tai chi class. I had learnt what I could from the practices yet I still wanted more, so I returned two years later to the Swamis Satchidananda and Devi Dhyani to continue with the second half of the energy enhancement course. On the first course I had received my first reiki one initiation but since two years had elapsed my teacher decided to redo the first initiations of level one before continuing with the other initiations reiki two and mastership. Mastership was left open, as it was not known if I would be ready for it.

It was a combination of the course that my reiki initiations and mediations were so powerful. After the first few sessions In Argentina I had to ask for a break, as the energies were too high. They had gradually increased in intensity. Initially I felt I was levitating off the chair, later it was off the ground and when I felt I was floating around the room, I had to call a halt. I felt if the door was opened I would float away like a helium balloon. With a short break the energies were able to realign themselves and calm down enough for me to continue. It is only by personally experiencing these energies that you can actually know what they do. It was good to gain new experience, get to grips with the energies and learn how to use them.

I gained Reiki Mastership by the end of the course and returned home looking for volunteers to practice on. Friends and acquaintances come forward with a variety of physical, mental, emotional and spiritual problems. Reiki is a channelling of the universal energy into the person receiving it, it is up to their body how much it receives and where it sends it to in the body for healing. The practioner is just the channeller and does not direct the energy; she/he allows the healing to take place on whichever level it is needed, be it emotional, physical or mental. During a treatment you place your hands and symbols in different parts of the body, so it was my learning process to read or feel what my hands were experiencing whilst doing this. Listening to what they were trying to tell me, the way I do this is being aware of the different energies that pass between my hands. Whether there is a good connection, what sort of energy is passing between, is it bumpy, smooth, twirling, zigzagging? A whole new world of communication was opening up to me; I had to learn a new energy language. I was looking to learn similarities, recurring sensations through my hands, continually asking what my hands were communicating to me, how would I know intuitively where more healing was required.

Over time and with continual practice I realised if healing was needed more in a particular area then more energy would be drawn through my hands, I could feel it travelling down my arms and into my hands for healing to take place. As the energies flow through me there is a whole communication between them and the person receiving treatment. The energies know where to go and I can be the silent witness, watching and learning.

How you might ask do I know these energies work? I can only answer that I know from the feedback I have had from those that received treatment. I have been truly gratified to see it work in so many ways and to help people make changes in their lives that really have made a difference. What has made the most impact on me is that it has opened other people's eyes to the reality that there is a spiritual side to their nature. It has opened a window to their true nature that was previously closed and can never be shut again.

As my awareness of the energies increased I wondered if different techniques could be introduced to increase their effectiveness. I found the energies could express themselves, if they approved of something. If I picked up a spiritual book the energy in my arm would increase. I noticed with my Sanskrit lessons the energies increased on hearing particular words. Even being close to certain people the energies would react, which would lead to question why it was so, normally it was because they were more spiritually evolved. It has been a huge communication channel that has opened up for me; my knowing comes from personal experience. I have also had the opportunity whilst teaching in meditation groups to be told when the energies pass through another person, so I know it is not just me experiencing them. Teaching is a wonderful sharing experience where there is not the pupil and teacher, just the teaching where both can learn. These same energies can even be carried through the written word as I write.

When I have said to people the energies have coursed down my arms, making the hairs stand up on end as though drawn to static, or it has felt like electricity sparking down my arms, I get blank looks. Occasionally I meet someone else who has experienced similar sensations and I find it gratifying I am not alone.

For me the energies are proof. They are something that I can physically work with to help others, this has provided a new and unexpected communication channel. It is early days in my learning process and I hope that the energies will teach me a lot more. These dancing energies are just the outer shell to the nut of spirituality that lies within.

My experience of spiritual energy has been pieced together over several years of personal experience and I felt it important to share my understanding of it before I take you back to where it all began in earnest on the energy enhancement course in Spain.

Chapter 15

Spain

As I travelled out to Spain in the Spring of 2003, I was wondering what I was actually letting myself in for. I really knew very little about the swamis I was due to meet. I had gone on instinct, quickly booked everything and headed off. On the flight to Girona I battled with my doubts and hesitation. At that time I was struggling to understand what being spiritual was all about. Way back in the year 1998 whilst on retreat I experienced satori for the first time, a state of sheer beauty beyond imagination and words. That was the real beginning of my spiritual search as I wished to repeat the experience. Such experiences might only occur once in a lifetime and the rest is just down to continual practice. Having felt this experience I was getting slightly despondent about my practice at home and by working with new techniques I hoped that my spiritual development might be quickened. I was determined to be open to what was offer and not prejudge or close myself down, to really trust the process and go with the flow

As I walked through the airport doors I easily spotted my Swamis Satchidananda and Devi Dhyani (Satchi and Devi) standing by the handrail at arrivals in Girona airport. They were distinctive in appearance and were not likely to blend into a crowd. I had seen photos of them but they had seen none of me, so I went up to them saying 'I believe you are looking for me?' I was warmly greeted by them and a fellow woman companion who was on the course. They were all very relaxed and open to chat to, as we ran through the usual pleasantries and journey details. We were near Girona's city centre so it was decided to pay a short visit to the old part for a wander around. As we did, it struck me we were just like ordinary tourists seeing the sights and taking photos but this was to turn out to be a very extraordinary visit for me.

Satchi started as he meant to go on in the car, it was all about raising our energies and busting our blockages, including our egos. He played some stimulating Santana music, it was far too loud for my liking as I always like to drive in silence, but I was too polite to complain. It was early days and I had not worked them out yet. I later found out it was their initial technique of bring blockages to the fore, a taste of things to come. Their aim was to activate our energy bodies to allow us to benefit from their existing energy field.

Satchi was a large and imposing man with long flowing blond hair and beard to match. He had kind eyes and a soft caring voice. I later found out I was just a few months older than him, which absurdly made me feel more mature. He loved intelligent conversation and challenging arguments. In the first week I sat back and listened to him and my lady companion discussing all manner of issues. For me it was very novel, as family life never presented me with an opportunity for intelligent conversation. Nobody ever asked my opinion or views on any thing important. I am not talking about what was on the television or in the newspaper but bigger, wider issues on the meaning of a spiritual life etc. In the second week when I was on my own with him it was very stimulating to have such conversations and slowly as we got to know each other, a close rapport built up. I felt he was like a cousin to me whom I could be familiar with and tease about personal or family matters and at the same time challenge his more outlandish ideas, yet all the time respecting him as a teacher.

His wife, Devi, was very different whilst he was an extrovert she was the opposite, she had a lovely serenity about her. She was an Argentinean lady with dark flamenco looks. Her English was perfect but as she spoke softly you had a job hearing and often had to ask her to repeat things. She had a sharp sense of humour, which was sometimes hard to catch onto. There is a rare breed of person who are born spiritual and she was one of these. I felt she had inborn natural powers and psychic vision but she kept them to herself, never advertising the fact. I appreciated her quiet manner and with each passing day I was able to learn something new from her. She had been a barrister before by profession and by using energy enhancement techniques had halved the time of her study and passed her exams, achieving so much in a short time

They lived in a rented villa in a small coast village in Catalonia. It was plainer and more basic than my imagination had led me to believe and I was grateful to have my own room. Mind you I did not have much time to spend in it except for sleeping. The plumbing in the place was appalling; I think it was there to test my patience and ego. In fact I do not know how I could mention it whilst talking about my spiritual quest but it did it annoy me and illustrated my struggle to overcome my annoyance, to go beyond it to acceptance.

Every morning you had to get up at six, no problem, then shower. First you had to try and ignite the boiler and get the flame going. Needless to say it never did, as my temper rose and before the swearing wanted to begin, it started. Into the bathroom, to get the hot water through you had to run a sink of hot water first, and then it went into the showerhead. I used to leap under it quick to catch the hot water and then it would immediately turn cold, normally my hair was full of shampoo by this time. Boy did I want to call it all manner of names. 'Was I such a wimp that I could not take a cold shower each morning to avoid the daily palaver?' I asked myself. I knew the swamis would be working on my ego to get me to realise its obstructiveness yet I never expected a shower to be my teacher, it was my bane. I could drop my ego and obey Satchi's instructions but that shower was a different matter. Satchi would refer to problems as challenging not difficult and that shower was very challenging for me.

It is a big learning curve practicing obedience to a guru. There is always a point at which you think to yourself why should I obey this when I do not think I should or I don't think this is right or necessary. Then the work begins to overcome one's resistance to it. With a guru you could possibly venture to argue against it at your own risk but with a shower you cannot do so, it is far more unmovable and illustrates one's own stubbornness clearly.

I did often mutter a few minor complaints when I received hard to apply instructions from the swami but he would reply 'why complain' and after a while I thought to myself that really there was no point in complaining, it was getting me nowhere. In fact it made me look foolish for doing so. I think at this point I should make it obvious that I am not a person who likes to be told what to do, I like to do things in my own way and be left alone to do quickly and efficiently. Woe be tide anyone who tells me to the contrary. I realise I have as big an ego as anybody else and it needs to be tackled daily, if I am to lessen its hold.

Humility is not a word that is used much today. To be humble does not mean to be a doormat. When I have seen humility in spiritual people it is reverential and beautiful, it is honouring something greater than yourself. You are part and parcel of it; in fact it is honouring something special within yourself. It is a respect for yourself and others, which comes from the soul. So often humble people have great gifts to share but they never boast or brag about them but silently go about giving them. It is deeply affecting to see humility in action. The word aspiration comes to mind; to aspire to humility is uplifting. In a world full of greed and envy, we need to raise our souls up and refine its good qualities. It is not just for ascetics but for everybody, otherwise why would it be a human quality in the first place. Humility can help loosen the shackles of daily life and ease it's stresses.

My first dispute with the swami came when he said sit cross legged with your knees touching the ground, my immediate response was 'I can't', plus the thought 'you must be joking'. My knees had never been able to touch the ground and I could never sit in a cross legged position for long. But sit I had to and after two weeks I could easily sit like it for an hour at a time. It just goes to show what a block the ego can be, what a hindrance in fact.

So the task was undertaken to learn the energy enhancement techniques that were proffered and learn I did. The course is all about learning to access and use universal energies. To purify your body and mind in order to progress on a spiritual life.

Although the course was very intensive we were allowed our more relaxing moments. My fellow lady companion and I headed off for the beach at the first opportunity. As we started to chat, we realised the more amusing aspects to the course, that if an outsider was watching us, they would think we were crazy. As we began to itemise particular examples we laughed at the absurdity of how we would seem, we laughed till tears ran down our faces. We were not a couple of weirdos but normal people, who had entered an unusual world. It was good to see a lighter side to it and we needed the release that laughter gave but inwardly we knew the seriousness of it and duly respected that. I was truly grateful for her company that first week and was sorry to see her leave.

In the first week we had been taught that people can sap other peoples energies, unintentionally and unknown to themselves. It just happens out of awareness. I vaguely understood what the swami was talking about, as you know that feeling of being drained after you have been with a particular person. We were taught techniques how to avoid this and to protect our own energies from being drained but it was not until I stood at the station waving goodbye to my companion that I fully understood. As she was walking away from me I could actually see a black sheet of energies being pulled from me by her. They were as large as my torso and went to a fine point towards her, I could physically feel its parting and just stood and watched. It all happened in a moment and was gone. I told the swami later and he confirmed that is what actually did happen. By living in the energy field of the two swamis my psychic vision was increased so that I was able to gain such an insight. It was personally able to witness what we had theoretically talked about, my understanding was greatly increased. The whole point of the course was to experience things personally and then you 'knew' they were real. You can often doubt yourself on the spiritual path questioning 'did I imagine it?' 'Or was it real?' Only direct experience confirms its reality.

As an aide to understanding what was real and what was not we were asked to write a testimonial of those experiences just as they happened.

Chapter 16

Testimonial from Spain

A requisite of the Energy Enhancement course was to write a testimonial of the events that occurred personally to oneself over the period of the course. Testimonials were posted on the website to show what actually happens on the courses. They are just factual accounts of what occurred and it is good to have them written down, as the memory is sometimes short and evasive. Often I look back and wonder 'did that really happen to me?' but as it stares back at me in black and white I know them to be true. What follows is my short summary of the time I spent out in Spain, starting with Level 1.

Having done meditation for some time and especially when I am on my own, I take the soft option when taking my sitting position. I was in for a rude awakening when I started my first meditation session with Satchi. Both knees had to be on the floor, which took several cushions beneath me. My spine had to be straight, chest expanded and pushed upwards, shoulders back, chin down. I realised I had not been sitting in a proper position for years and this was difficult. I had been doing hatha yoga for the past twelve years.

During the past two years when I meditated, I have twirled like a top when my bottom came into contact with the floor. Satchi explained this was the Kundalini rising and I needed to find the centre of it. By swaying backwards and forwards, then side to side, I could touch upon its centre but it is a very fine place to contact and I had kept going off course. The same movement was to be done with my head, keeping the chin down. Then I needed to keep rechecking throughout the meditation to find that central point again. Achieving the correct sitting position I was able to move on.

The course was a blockage-busting course. We are full of negative emotions, thoughts, feelings, and memories from the past that keep us small and hinder our spiritual growth. We replay outdated behaviour and habits that do us no favours. Energy enhancement techniques allow these negative energies to be seen as blockages to ones spiritual growth and offer techniques to eliminate them for good out of ones life. Blockages can be held in the body and one evening whilst meditating, as I was focusing on my stomach blockage I got distracted by a bad cough and had to leave the room. Satchi explained the belly and throat chakras were connected, hence my cough. Distraction has to be caught early on, that was why I had stopped meditating. In bed that night on another try, I was enjoying the white light so much I did not feel like following the sequence and wanted to remain in the white light. I fell sleep but was awoken by a loud popping sound and an image of a black disc, which was a negative blockage releasing itself. Often whilst in meditation I saw blockages as black coal or oil and when I burnt it would cause heat to flow back up the spine. It was a continual process of doing the techniques and experiencing the results. More congruently emotions or feelings would arise during meditation such as grief or sadness and these I sent down to be destroyed. Past events could naturally surface to one's mind then be eliminated; it was all part of the clearing process. To become spiritual you have to clear negative thoughts, emotions and feelings in order to create the space for the spiritual presence to flow in. To make the space.

Once I was trying this process I became angry, I knew I did not want my blockages anymore, that was why I had come on the Energy Enhancement course, I was fed up with them, they had served no purpose for me so far in my life, they had done me no good I wanted rid of them. I threw them in the fire with venom, as I started to throw, I wanted to throw more on. I became very angry. I felt I had so much to be angry about; I could go on forever. After this session I felt quite good. Satchi said I would need to carry this same practice for quite a while and should practice at every opportunity in order to get rid of all my blockages and practice I did.

As I moved onto completing level two, I continued with the following testimonial.

I have been asked to write down what I have achieved so far from the powerful techniques Energy Enhancement Level 2. As it will be helpful on my return home when I become distracted by my everyday life. I seem to have two separate lives, one with family, and the other spiritual. I now need to integrate the two, with the focus on my spiritual path. In the past I have let the family override it but now I am aware of it I can do something about it. I no longer need to be a victim of circumstance. I can take control of my own destiny.

If only it were that easy, I have learnt on the EE course about negative energies that stop this. They are also the same energies that make me have a lack of energy most of the time and have also caused my skin problem. Through EE I have realised these have been very detrimental to me as a person, they are outmoded and have had a very damaging effect on my life. I want to eliminate them from my life.

Strategies are so ingrained and resistant to change that I will need to continually use the EE techniques to banish them. Once I realised how harmful they were, I became more determined to tackle them. I have been taught that they react when they are threatened, so I have to be vigilant as to their cunning ways. I have found the Poor

Me pops up to say 'you are no good at this, why bother?' or the Self Destructor, who makes my skin more itchy just when I think its healing, the list can go on. Disappointment and amnesia are also tools used by the strategies to stop ones development, both of which have arisen during the course and Satchi was able to nip them in the bud and point them out to me.

Through out the course I have been taught to listen to my body, where is the ache or pain, this indicates where the blockage is that needs to be worked on. During meditation, blockages also appeared as small black discs. This is an area that I have worked continually on with EE techniques every day. During meditation sessions I felt popping in different parts of my body, and over the last two weeks I have felt an increase in health and vitality, as blockages have been removed. Similar sensations of release have also been felt in my stomach area where I have had past problems.

The EE course has given me a clearer understanding of my blockages; during meditation I have felt a vice like grip in my heart chakra. I knew before I came on the course that this was a major area that I needed to work on. Two years ago in Greece it came to light that I thought myself unlovable and I was dumbfounded. I could love others easily but I did not love myself. I have been working on it ever since. I wonder if everyone suffers from this too but it is deeply buried in our psyche, hence we always seek a partner to love and be loved.

I now know I am deeply loved by the light and it will guide my life, if I let it. For many years I have had hints of what my life path would be but I have played the strategies of poor me and the self destructor. Thinking I am not good enough or able. I was sitting on the cliff the other day and a minute ant bit my foot, I thought if that small ant could make me jump, what could I achieve? Satchi has

made me aware that the strategies will try again to play themselves through me, to sabotage my hopes and dreams, so I have to be alert to them.
I often find that the white light comes easier to me at night. On one particular night near dawn, when I was awake my whole life fell into place. Everything I had done so far and everyone I had met led me to this moment in time. It had all been useful, good and bad to lead me to this moment of being on the course and fulfilling my life path.

Surprisingly it is my skin complaint of 18 years that has propelled me along my path. I have travelled through the maze of many alternative therapies and gained an insider knowledge of them. Gaining more desperate as the time has gone by, with no cure, I felt learning EE would help it. Satchi and Devi over the last two weeks have continually worked on it with me. Devi has prescribed herbs and oil that I have been taking. I have also been receiving Reiki healing from her and doing it myself as she taught me.

Its funny how one thing leads to another, learning Tai Chi led to a spiritual healer, where I gained personal experience of it. Taking an Open University degree course led me onto a Diploma in Counselling. Failing the final section of the course led to personal centred art therapy then onto actually learning to draw and paint myself. Fundraising led to teaching myself computer, advertising and publicity skills. Yoga postures led to meditation and seeking out various teachers. A meditation teacher, led me to creative writing by questioning what did I really want to do and I replied write. Voluntary work has put in contact with a wide range of people with courses following on so that I could help more. The list goes on, it makes me realise that there is a greater force playing through my life. I hope one day to write a book about it.

Another night after I had been in the light, I had a very clear dream of a multi faceted diamond that reflected the light. I asked the light who or what this was, the reply was that it was myself. I asked what was its purpose and the reply was so that I could reflect the light, that the light would shine through me. It has always been my hope that the light would shine through my work and that I could touch people's hearts so that they would know that the light existed and that it would deeply affect and help them.

I know I can now travel up to the white light in the centre of the universe and form a connection with the core of the earth. It did not happen easily, as I had blockages that had to be worked on before I could connect. Now the white light is all pervading and I can feel the Kundalini rise up from the bottom of my spine.

This has been a blockage busting course, I have had to face the multitude of fears that have kept me small, the task to eliminate them will be ongoing. The mind's a killer but I have been given the tools to tackle all negative thought forms. I have also tackled present life experience blockages in a similar manner. My dependency on alcohol has been detrimental to my health and needed to be unblocked. There are also a lot of inner children that have to be dealt with, but first things first, I am tackling the strategies, as Satchi says " by accentuating the positive and eliminating the negative".

I have been given the necessary tools to use in my everyday life to further me on my spiritual quest. My knowledge has been greatly increased in the area of herbalism, homeopathy, acupressure, all of which are more effective with the EE techniques. I have been shown the necessary yoga positions to focus upon to combat poor posture and the healing of a past shoulder injury. At the end of the course I can even keep my knees on the floor in meditation for an hour at a time now, showing the unblocking work done on my base chakra has been successful and I am gaining a better understanding of the energies all round.

I have been taught to test for pesticides in my food and understand the effect they are having on my health and the environment. I have been given methods to eliminate toxins when they are in my system. I have also been shown how to cook healthy energising food that will improve my life.

Devi has given me Reiki I and 2 initiations, which have been beautiful experiences and I will be able to practice them with those in need.

Satchi and Devi have given so much of themselves that I do not know where to begin. Their care and love has been with me throughout the past two weeks for which I am eternally grateful. They have openly shared their special gifts and knowledge, filtering into my life to make it more whole, which has helped me progress on my spiritual path far quicker than I expected.

Chapter 17

Stillness

I thought I knew what stillness was until I really experienced it for the first time. It slowly crept up on me whilst I was staying with the two swamis in Spain. Between them they create a higher energy field in which to do their work and students who come to stay with them have to become used to it. To be able to function within it and to use the increased energies to accentuate their learning.

One afternoon I went out on the balcony and surveyed the scene in front of me, nothing different about the fir trees surrounding the villa or the street of houses in front of me. It was more that I sensed a strong feeling of stillness all around. Everywhere was like an auditorium of stillness, rather like after a beautiful piece of music. The pause before the applause. Only this was much deeper. Initially I thought it must be my imagination playing tricks, then my mind started to rationalise it. The two swamis I was living with would naturally project an aura of stillness around them but I remained unconvinced. It had nothing to do with them; it was so called out there. The fir trees exuded stillness, the road was serene with it, the overlooking houses acknowledged it. Stillness was everywhere, it was very solid and tangible.

Over the forthcoming days I kept returning to the same spot to check it out, I tried it from different perspectives, I stood under the trees, I walked on the road and yes it was still there. I filed these memories away at the back of my mind as just one of the many experiences I had whilst there.

It was only when I returned home and was amazed at the stillness

I found in my garden, that I tied it together. I wanted to exclaim this stillness for all to know. The same sense of stillness pervaded everywhere, in the house I could gaze in awe at the stillness of a table or a plant. It was as though they had the gift of stillness all along and I only just now recognised it. The stillness has a strength and serenity to it, its immovable and unchanging. It was always there and will always be so; the difference was that I could now connect with it.

Even in the noisiest places, beyond all the hustle and bustle there is stillness and I can be blown away by it when I feel it. Meditation has quietened my mind enough to allow that connection to take place. I never set out to find stillness; if I had, I'm sure it would have eluded me. It crept up on me unawares. People like to sit in churches to feel the stillness that exists within the walls, it feels like the stillness that has built up over many years and permeates there. But that same stillness is around us all the time, it never goes away, it is never diminished or reduced; it's just there. You sense stillness whereas initially I could see it. My guru told me that it was a reflection of the stillness I had inside, the stillness we all have inside if we can tune into it. You can use all of your senses to experience the silence within.

Besides stillness itself you can sense silence in stillness. When I first started meditating I complained to my guru that silence was so loud, like the background fizzle on a radio. I was told it was space expanding. As I was tuning my ears into the silence the noise seemed to increase, when I paid less attention to hearing and just being aware it decreased.

First your body then your mind has to be still in order to access silence. Over the years of meditating and accessing silence daily I cannot expound its wonders enough. Silence is supportive and loving. You are never alone with silence, it contains so much, silence can help you through those difficult times in life when events seem unbearable, it never disappears and is always waiting for you. Silence is within and without, you are never separate from it. It calms and heals, to rest in it is joyful and I wanted others to benefit in the same way as I had done so I started to teach meditation.

I teach meditation from my home and as we live in the countryside, I am very fortunate to have a garden surrounding the house.

Chapter 18

Garden

Unbeknown to me the first noticeable experience of silence and stillness, was when I was doing my gardening. I naturally slipped into a place of no mind when I was working with the plants and soil. I was carrying out the activity but as I was totally absorbed in my task it allowed an opening up of my being. Initially I did not realise what had happened I would have described it as a feeling of 'lost in space', which in fact is just what it is.

I had my first experience of gardening when I was eight years old when my Dad reluctantly gave me a small space from his vegetable patch in the back garden. We had moved into our new council house when I was five, I watched my father create two small lawns with rose beds surrounding them and a vegetable plot out the back. For my Dad it was a wish come true having the opportunity to till the soil so to speak. Like all new houses the garden was a dumping ground for all the builders rubble but that did not deter his spirit as he brought out an ancient spade of his father's and started to turn the earth over.

I could feel his satisfaction when the first spikes of green protruded from the newly sewn lawn. On the first try at planting grass you are never sure if the seeds will take and it seems a miracle when they do. Forty years later I went through the same process of hope and physical labour.

My mother still has the Queen Elizabeth standard rose that my Dad planted fifty years earlier and survived two house moves. I have the habit today that when I move house, it does not just mean the furniture but my favourite plants as well. It has been known for the compost heap to come too, much to the surprise of the removal men. In some respects my plants are my family, when I leave them behind I am hoping the next house dweller will appreciate their value and take good care of them. Our garden is the closest we can come to nature and watch its procreation first hand. A window box, or a patio plant can encourage birds and insects alike, bringing a small eco climate right under your nose. Through meditation I have been able to take time, stop and stare, to wonder at the tiniest of creatures on a plant. To study them in detail and marvel at God's creation, that such effort was taken to create such an intricate body. Tiny hairs on the thinnest of legs, beautiful iridescent colours on a bird's head are just a couple of the wonders to ponder upon.

I can see myself as a child in the open enjoying a ladybird, singing the verse 'ladybird, ladybird fly a way, come back another day'. The tending of my vegetable patch was intermittent and my Dad complained bitterly at the amount of weeds. Amongst them I did achieve the odd flower and so my love of gardening began. As the weeds took over my Dad reclaimed his piece of land back for more fruitful endeavours but not before I buried my burnt cakes from my first cooking attempt in it.

My initial adult foray into gardening was when we brought an old ex farm workers cottage on a dairy farm. Great I thought, no shortage of manure there and so I enthusiastically started a very large vegetable plot. It was a mammoth task clearing the brambles and weeds from the overgrown garden. I enlisted the help of any willing family members, including my grandmother. It was hard work but satisfying. With all that manure everything grew well including the slugs and worms, they thrived in the fertile soil and grew to the most ugly proportions but I persevered. As my family grew, the vegetable patch became dramatically reduced until it actually disappeared and was replaced by a swing and slide.

As the house was on a main road and with young children we were keen to move. The next time we chose a new home that needed no work on it and a small garden, which I was able to create around the house. From its small dimensions I found room for a mini orchard, rose garden, vegetable patch and two small patios. As it was a friendly small village the' Village Produce Association' had survived, a throw back to the war when growing fruit and vegetables were encouraged. Its members were hardcore gardeners who knew everything there was to know about gardening and they were a continual source of advice and guidance. They had their yearly flower and vegetable show where my small specimens sat beside their magnificent beans or sweet peas. I learnt to ask what they had done to achieve such results and they were always keen to tell their tales. Gardening to me had to fit around everything else and its main emphasis was somewhere to sit and enjoy the sun at any spare moment and a place for children to play in.

As my leisure time increased and I no longer had to do the school runs I had a resurgence of my dream of creating a large garden out of nothing. This coincided with the decision of moving house again. After the trials and tribulations of several deals falling through we ended up with a new house, which had half an acre of garden. As I cast my eyes over the builder's rubble and the size of the weeds I wondered just what I had let myself in for. Little did I realise that underneath the weeds lay large lumps of concrete, broken bricks, car windscreens, back axles, and old farming implements. It was a lucky dip every time I put my spade in.

As we moved in so did my plants and compost heap. I had been to the autumn sales at the garden centres and brought my shrubs and trees at reduced prices, all I had to do was plant them. That winter as I pondered over various plans for the garden, the heavy rains formed a natural pond in the clay soil at the back of the house and with it came the idea that the pond was to be there, where it could be viewed from all the back windows in the house. In fact the garden had the habit of telling me where it wanted things and as it backed on fields I wished it to be as natural as possible.

Come the spring we had to have the diggers and workmen in to level the ground, cut out the rockery and pond area and tear down some high fir trees. It was a relief to watch all the work being carried out, as we would never have been able to do it ourselves. They seeded the lawn area for us and as when I was a child I was delighted to see the haze of green spread over the soil as the first shoots came up.

As the spring moved towards summer I sent out an SOS to friends, relatives, neighbours of my parents, in fact anyone who might throw a plant out. I became a refuge for unwanted shrubs and plants. Buying them from nurseries was expensive and there was no the spare cash for them, so I looked for cheap smaller alternatives and had pleasure watching them grow. I took cuttings or seeds and started to reproduce my own, slowly over time my beds started to expand in size. At markets, fetes or garden sales I was always on the lookout for new varieties and yet again the sellers were pleased to help and give advice.

Gardening is a very acceptable topic of conversation in a village and when I was asked to open my garden as part of the Annual Open Garden Scheme, I thought that I might be able to share my own experiences with others and showing what could be achieved without too much expenditure. There were new housing developments in the village and I hoped my garden might provide an inspiration for those new to gardening or at the very least, give some new ideas. It was a very rewarding time where I think I learnt the most from all the visiting gardeners but it was very stressful preparing the garden for display. Somehow I had the idea that it needed to be weed free, with all the flowers standing upright and no greenfly. It was gratifying to share a love of gardening with so many people. Two years later I opened it again to show just how much the garden had grown and altered in the intervening time and many of those first visitors returned to see it.

There is something very basic about handling the earth and growing things in it. Even after hard toil you feel good about yourself despite the aches and pains. I have had to pick-axe most of my plants into the soil, digging out rubble and breaking down the hard lumps of clay. The effort is normally done with a lot of muttering and occasional swearing but when I see the plant growing, I get a sense of satisfaction that it is growing because of my own endeavours.

I cannot say when I realised my garden was my temple that I worshipped in. It was not the normal kind of worship where you sit down and pray. It was more of hands on experience. It was more than just being out in the open air, with the sky above you and the soil beneath. It was more than just experiencing the seasons first hand, the numbness of the cold in winter, the fresh sweat brought about by the sun in summer. It was more than just inhaling flower scents or the touch of soft green leaves on my skin. It was more than the freshness of morning dew or the crunch of frost under my feet. It was more than the twitter of birds feeding, the bees buzzing, the flutter of butterflies or the wildlife that came. Yes it was all of these but so much more.

As I spent more time in the garden I found I treated it like my sanctuary, a place I could go and be at peace whilst actually gardening. I became aware that when I was weeding or digging I entered into a very peaceful space. It has nothing to do with the sounds surrounding me; it was more of a journey inwards to find the silence within. Whilst physically carrying out my chores I was able to stop my mind chatter and just be aware of what I was doing. There was a connection between my eyes and hands that cut out any thoughts or feelings. I was able to deeply connect with what I was doing and gain a respite from my everyday cares. Unbeknown to me I was naturally entering into a meditative state when I was gardening and it was a good prelude to the discipline of practice I would have to follow. In fact it showed me that practice need not be disciplined, it could just happen naturally if you allowed it to do so.

It was a connection to the silence within, which provided a calm and serene presence. It came as a surprise that I had entered meditative awareness without my having to work towards achieving it. I entered a timeless space where I was totally oblivious yet encompassed by everything around me. It had completeness about it, that I was not separate from my garden or gardening, it was all part of the whole. This realisation expanding into, I was part of Nature, then the Universe, there was no separation. It is a rather difficult concept to explain and it was a slow realisation on my part, as for many years I was unaware of what was actually happening. Gardening gave me my first taste of meditation without me realising it. I found the stillness within and wanted it to become more a part of my life. I can only say that I became aware that I was in a meditative state when I came out of it, I realised I had no idea of where I had been or for how long I was there. It was encouraging that it had happened naturally and it was evidence that I could enter that state and had the ability to do so. Gardening gave me the first taste of meditation, which inspired me to learn more about it.

Gardening provided me with a restful place to recharge my soul. I often wonder how many other hobbies might provide the same restful place that we all can enter, be it fishing or reading. For me garden allowed a meditative state to arise naturally and when I started to meditate I had already experienced that space.

From gardening I developed an interest in growing herbs, as I knew little about them I researched them to understanding their medicinal uses. I was keen to use them on myself but hesitated that I might poison myself in the process. I felt more comfortable using them on my skin and as I had a skin complaint for over twenty years I had plenty of opportunity to do so.

Chapter 19

Surrender

There are many different ways to Self-awareness, some more surprising than others. I have never been the type of person to give in easily, in fact surrender is the antithesis to my nature, I would fight to the bitter end rather than surrender. Illness is a good teacher for learning the act of surrender.

On returning from a foreign holiday I broke out in horrendous sores, mainly on my legs and arms. Some were over an inch in diameter and they were very weepy and raw. As my immune system tried to get into gear to overcome it, I became exhausted and tired, I could do nothing but sleep. Fortunately I did not have a high temperature or feel sick, I just had no energy at all. I couldn't stand for long so I was quite happy to stay in bed and rest. I had no choice but to surrender to the illness and let my body fight it off on its own. I had to tend the sores and eat but apart from that I wanted to do nothing. For two weeks I gave in to it, I slept most of the time but in the times in between I took the opportunity to meditate and turn inwards. I would not dwell on my predicament but turn inwards. Even waking at night I did the same practicing with the various meditation methods I had been taught.

It had often been my habit up till then to practice at night if I woke up, instead of tossing and turning trying to get to sleep I would, either get up, sit and meditate or do a relaxation technique in bed. Either way I would be ready afterwards to go back to sleep or at the very least I had been doing something useful. I'd been taught to do relaxation before sleeping and focusing on spiritual reading in the morning before getting up, so it seemed quite natural to do the same if the opportunity arose in between sleeping. In this way semi consciously I was able to drop into the white light occasionally and I have tried to build on this further. My illness and state of surrender allowed a deepening of my meditation process, it was a space for it to happen without my doing anything to achieve it.

I was taking homeopathic medicine at the time and was prepared to give it a good go but after the two weeks the sores became infected and more broke out. I had to turn to conventional medicine and much against my wishes used antibiotics and steroids, I could not live any more with the erupting Vesuvi on my body. I had viewed them as nature's way of eliminating the toxins from my body but when they turned septic I had to review my diagnosis. The last thing I wanted was blood poisoning. I then had to go to a consultant and follow his recommended course of action. There had been so many consultants over the years and so many failed attempts at a cure. How many strong drugs is one prepared to take in the hope of a cure? Yet again I found myself willing to take a powerful drug that was used for cancer in the very hope of that illusive cure.

The skin condition I have had for twenty years has been my teacher, surrender has just been one of the many things I have had to learn over the years. I had perfect skin up until I gave birth to my second child. I was anaemic at the time and after the birth my blood would not clot and I needed a transfusion. It wasn't until six months later that I noticed an itching on the bottom of my feet. I was out to dinner at the time and the itching became so intense I had to remove my shoe and go for it. I then noticed my fellow dinners staring at me and that was the start of it.

Small blister like lumps rose up under the skin and itched like mad until I scratched them till they bled. My father, husband and children always tried to get me to stop but if you have an itch you know it won't disappear until its been scratched. I think you could have held me down forcefully and I would still have found a way to scratch. The blisters spread up my legs and multiplied; then onto my hands and arms and later my body. In my ears, hair, lower regions, nowhere was itch free. I saw consultant after consultant, they all had their own ideas, it wasn't eczema or psoriasis but they would never admit it baffled them. I tried all manner of drugs, getting stronger and stronger with each failed attempt. Many violently upset my stomach until I had to say no more. Twice lumps were cut out from me. First I had a lovely operating theatre, but the second time I had to just lay my arm across the doctor's stomach whilst he cut one out. I went in front of a team of skin specialists who peered at me intently and shook their heads. By then I had reached they end of conventional medicine and turned to alternative ones.

The thing with a skin condition is, it is noticeable enough for people to comment on and comment they do, mainly its a kind hearted offer of advice, 'have I tried such and such?' And try them I did. I would try anything as I got more desperate. I cannot believe I actually grew some horrid mould in the airing cupboard and drank it every day! I have stuck marigolds onto my legs, I have rubbed raw aloe vera into the sores. I have tried everything that was suggested to me. I think I could write a book on it just alone but none of it really helped.

A nutritionalist cured my irritable bowel but not my skin. I had to go on a stone age diet for six weeks which was very minimal and basic, then slowly reintroduce various foods. To date I try to avoid wheat and dairy products as much as possible. I also took mineral supplements that I was missing, especially zinc which my body was not absorbing. So that was a benefit of one treatment.

Normally every alternative therapist I tried, would be for a year at least. This included a hynotherapist, Chinese herbalists, reflexologist and homeopaths. I have brought myself books on

Accupressure and Accu-yoga, Shiastsu to teach myself.

My skin has taught me perseverance, to never give up hope and things have slowly improved but not gone away. I have had to face my skin condition being visible. It has made me feel dirty and ashamed, wearing trousers and long sleeved clothes allowed most of it to go unnoticed but it always remained visible on my hands. I used to have to say to myself over and over again 'I am not a skin condition', 'I have one but it is not me'. I was not going to let it spoil my life and make me into a recluse.

It gave me great empathy for those who have disfigurements and have to face the public. They are not their disability, they just have one. So often we allow the disability to cover the person underneath and that's very sad because the person has a lot to contend with. I greatly admire their bravery in getting on with their lives and not letting the disability or prejudice get in their way. I always felt I should apologise for my skin especially when I was preparing food for the elderly or children's parties. I wanted to explain that it wasn't catching or harmful, often I was too shy or ashamed to say anything and prayed it would not be noticed. Perhaps I was just too self-conscious of it, I have been only shown concern.

Just when I thought it was getting a bit better and was looking less obvious. I was sitting on a park bench in London when a tramp appeared, talking noisily to himself. I shrunk inside and wished him not to sit next to me, he sat on a bench nearby. The next thing I know he is trying to catch my attention for a chat and asked did I have eczema. I was flabbergasted that he knew and so he progressed to saying how bad he and his sister had it, their history and problems. It was heart warming we were able to share our problem and I felt belittled that I initially wanted to avoid him from my first assumption that he was drunk.

I have met many people with skin problems and we have been able to share our feelings about it. This has also formed a link to many other people's problems and so that we all share suffering in our lives. Suffering is a human condition. I have been far too quick to make the assumption that I know what someone suffers without really knowing. I need to hear their own story, how it affects their life and how they relate to it. Each one is different and unique.

So my skin condition has also taught me patience, twenty years is a long time to be patient and I have had to maintain hope throughout it all that a cure can be found. I have tremendous respect for my skin, they way it heals and replenishes itself is amazing. It has opened up my thinking about disease, I have had to challenge if I had psychologically brought it on myself. I was most appalled when a consultant came to the conclusion I was not a self harmer. Did he think I would voluntarily do this to myself? One benefit of seeing a specialist is that they look with interest at your skin and run their hands over your lumps and bumps. Perversely that simple touch reaches deeply into me. Often he has been the only one to touch them and somehow it makes you grateful they do. It has made me realise touch can be a powerful healer.

It was always my hope that eventually I would find a cure for my skin complaint, I reasoned that if I tried hard enough and looked at every available alternative therapy the answer would be found. I never found that miraculous cure I hoped for but it has taught me the valuable lesson of surrender, there are some things that cannot be changed, they have to be surrendered to. Yes you do everything in your power to aid healing and not aggravate it but there comes a point when you have done everything you possibly can and you have to just accept it as it is.

Meditation had greatly eased the irritation of my skin. When I was out in Spain with the Swamis I noticed a great improvement on my skin but when I came back home it returned to how it was. There were the ups and downs of it generally, some more severe than others. It was linked into stress and hormonal changes as well as being tied into the seasons. Come autumn it would start to decline and in the summer it would improve but never disappeared for long. I learnt to live with it but I never gave up hope of a cure, with this in mind I returned to the Swamis in Argentina to continue learning energy enhancement, but still at the back of my mind I hoped a side benefit would be the healing of my skin.

Chapter 20

Argentina testimonial

It was over two years before I decided to return to complete the second part of the Energy Enhancement course. I was still battling with my skin complaint and was having difficulties in my life, when suddenly I felt the time was right. My husband booked the flight and we headed off half way around the world, all within a matter of weeks. What follows is the testimonial I wrote then.

Two years previously I completed the first half of the energy enhancement course in Spain with Satchi and Devi. In one respect it seems just yesterday but in another a life time away. A lot has happened in my life between that time deaths, births, daughter's marriage, ill health; the usual variety of life's traumas. I returned from the first course full of determination to follow my spiritual path, I was going to do such great things but being a wife and mother just took over. At the times when I most needed to practice I did not, which in turn lead to much inner suffering. I was also struggling to get myself acknowledged as a spiritual person by those close to me. I was tired of living two lives, one as a family person and the other as a spiritual one. To incorporate the two was no easy task and relationship problems developed which is what really brought me back to the course. I needed ways of dealing with relationships close to me. I had enough of being drawn into emotional traumas and expectations. I needed the tools to develop non attachment, whilst at the same time being more open and loving. I needed a better understanding of how to stop my energies from being drained from me and I came back to the course as I needed to find the answers.

I knew the format of the course, we were given an initiation into a new technique and then it was up to us to practice it. I was meditating up to six hours a day and I experienced new kinds of meditative states that I had not previously known. If I had been told that I would have to sit and meditate that long I would have thought it was an impossibility. Being over fifty and not used to sitting on the floor, I had great difficulty in sitting cross-legged. I tried for an hour, wriggled, stretched, retried, gave-up. I admired a fellow young man sitting bolt upright in the full lotus opposite me. I reasoned he was well under half my age and his legs were still supple. It was stressed by Satchi the need for being crossed legged in order to free up the blockages in our legs and help to open the base chakra. We witnessed the same young man when his base chakra did open and boy did he know it from the great heat it generated. When he explained his experience and the sensations he felt, it had the wow factor about it. He said it felt like a flower opening, which created much mirth during translation. He was an inspiration and I continued to endeavour sitting cross legged, over the days that passed, the time I could sit like that went on for longer and the pains grew less.

By getting the physical body aligned and the spine acting as an aerial for the energies, my meditation improved. The aim was to transmit energies from the highest source available therefore I had to reach these levels before I could access them. As each day passed I pushed myself higher to the centre of the Universe and beyond. It was quite a challenge, part of me understanding the concept and willing to try, the other part not knowing what to expect. It is only experiencing them that one can acknowledge their reality, everything is experiential, only believing when you experience it first hand.

As the energies grew in strength I learnt to trust them and become accustomed to them but I questioned what was the point of my experiencing them. I asked for the energies to teach me what I needed to know. I asked to gain knowledge and wisdom to understand what was being taught me by their presence. I was there to learn, to be receptive to what was offered.

I felt energised by the process, at times I felt as though my bottom would lift me off the floor. That progressed to my feet wanting to do vertical take off and it got to a stage where I felt woozy and dizzy with the energies. I felt like a hot air balloon that needed to be tied down or I would drift way. I was told I would only be given that which I could deal with but I felt I was up to my maximum capacity. In meditation plate shifts occurred, tornadoes whirled through my body as I continued to meditate. What was the point of all this? I questioned what was I meant to do with it all. There would be no point in me returning to my life acting as though I was on some drugs spaced out. How would people react to me? What would I have achieved? So many questions to be answered. I kept coming back to the challenge of balancing my family life with my spiritual life, how to incorporate the two.

The two year gap had been beneficial in that I came with a renewed conviction to learn and develop from what was being taught. I had found I tended to live an insular spiritual life at home, although I was able to learn from the gurus and swami's I mixed with. I was pleased to join an on going group in Argentina half way through; I was welcomed and made to feel a part of it immediately. The group provided a valuable learning environment as its members explained their personal experiences, as previously on my own I often wondered was it just me who felt like this. I was deeply touched by their commitment and determination to follow a spiritual path despite all the difficulties. The benefit of the course is the tackling of shared difficulties, as well as learning new techniques.

By experiencing the energies it was proof that they existed, I visited spaces of beauty and serenity. A place where total freedom was experienced. There were places of no feeling, no emotions, a place of respite and calm. I was encouraged to reach my maximum capacity. I could have sat for many years at home never touching these places but there came a point when I knew I needed that extra push and I was given the opportunity on the course. Having worked with Satchi previously I knew I could trust him and that he held the interests of all his students' dear to him. He was not about to abuse my trust, he knew when to push or goad and when to encourage and praise. I could still openly disagree with him without the harmony being disrupted.

Before I left home I was prepared to be open to what was being given and not to make any prejudgements, to be open to new relationships with others and try new things out. A major hope was that my intuition would be enhanced and as the time passed on the course I could feel myself intuitively understanding the whole person that stood in front of me. With the language separation I could see this more clearly at work. Devi kindly translated all that was taught into Spanish and the Spanish questions back into English in order that everyone could understand. When I was spoken to in Spanish about some complex matter, I could intuitively react back without knowing what was being said. The language problem seemed no barrier at all other than I could not express myself with words. There was also the age difference as I was the oldest by far of the students, yet I did not feel this. I was openly accepted as to who I was, even though I walked in on the course two weeks after it had started and was an unknown quantity, a grandmother from England. But we all shared spiritual aspirations, a yearning to learn and a commitment to our spiritual paths. We all desired this course to make a difference to our lives to aid our spiritual advancement.

Being in a group we learnt from each other and freely shared experiences. Another hope that I had from the course was I wanted to be inspired, to be able to use my initiative, to be able to inspire others to use the techniques in every day life. A young Argentinean man 20 years of age who was very committed to practising the techniques took them out into his home, his family relationships and his work. He told us both his parents and some friends had taken to using the practices. He illustrated the techniques actually worked, which in turn encouraged me. I also admired his sweet voice and disclosed to him how uncomfortable I felt with mine. 'just by practice it improves', he said simply. He was evidence as to the success of the methods taught as he too felt his voice inadequate but now he was able to play the guitar and sing in public, being a children's entertainer.

The course stimulated me to open my heart more. There was I on my first day wondering what I had let myself in for and the two weeks ahead lay like an untravelled empty road. I need not have feared I was greeted by several young Argentinean men giving kisses of greeting on both cheeks. Being British this was not something I was used to and I think I must have conveyed something of this by my body language. So they explained this was the natural way of greeting and leaving a person each time in Argentina. I felt at home immediately and learnt to go with the flow and be open to what was being given. Each had their own particular talents, which they easily shared. There was a natural warmth and affection that was given. Although each of our characters were very different there was a feeling of oneness where we acted as a unit. No discord ever arose as there was only harmony and we learnt from each other. Personal stories and experiences were shared in a caring environment. I felt myself accepted as I was and my confidence to be myself increased. A student asked to do a video recording of my spiritual journey to date and this was something I would never before have envisaged myself doing naturally. It was good to be with like-minded spiritual people who wanted to make a difference in this world; I was not alone or classed odd. It has been noted by the other group members that my appearance had improved in just one week and I felt the inner changes myself that had taken place. My energy levels were high, I have a lightness about my body and a tranquil calmness surrounding me.

Another Argentinean man had natural psychic abilities, he was quiet natured and said very little in the group sessions but over meal times his wife translated his intuitions to me in broken English and I got to understand and know him better. He taught me how to cleanse a room with reiki and regularly corrected my twirling techniques, all without the use of language. He and his wife were deeply spiritual and on the night of the full moon they became initiated as sannyasins (those that devote to a spiritual life). Devi our Reiki Master had created an altar on the rooftop decked with symbols, candles and flowers. Devi wore a magnificent purple cloak and presided over the ceremony whilst the two sannyasins knelt at her feet. It was an emotional and moving ceremony for them and I was privileged to be able to witness the depth of their commitment. They were given their spiritual names to be used from then onwards but there was a slight problem about the twins she was carrying in her belly so they were also named.

Humour and laughter was always around and there was a consensus to enjoy what was presented in life. I felt encouraged dropping my inhibitions and joining in with the dancing, singing, twirling and chanting, although my self-consciousness still loomed in the background. We worked and played together, yet we knew when it was right to meditate and practice and not waste valuable time.

As we meditated at every available opportunity, we did not have to be told to do so, if we had any spare time it would be spent in meditation tackling the blockages we had. Part of the course was to acknowledge and dissolve any avoidance strategies to practising. We were taught many techniques to identify and deal with strategies and inner children that sabotage ones life. It really seemed an unneeded process but I knew I needed to get as much work done as I could before returning home when practising would prove more difficult with the distractions of every day life.

I have been able to observe in myself avoidance techniques, resistances and ways that I act irrationally; all these point to blockages that have to be eliminated. I developed willpower to get rid of them as I was sick and tired of many of them adversely affecting my life and I wanted to be free of them. Getting angry with them increased my determination. I spent one session working on eradicating the sabotaging self-destructor and I was getting really mad using all the techniques to break it down. I created a bonfire on which to throw all my negativities and there were many, I continually fuelled it. I even took the bonfire to bed with me and left it burning all night at my bedside but after much determination and meditation I became free of it.

We later moved onto dealing with relationships, which was the main reason why I had gone on the course. I was having problems with those close to me not taking on board that I was on a spiritual path. It was a natural progression for me to do so but I felt those close to me had little understanding of what being spiritual meant. After being on the course I realised it was up to me to incorporate those people around me into my spiritual journey, so that we moved on together.

My endurance was continually being tested. When I reach the maximum of what I think I can suffer in a given situation, that boundary moved further away and then I struggle to reach that and then it moved on again. Until I find I have travelled a longer path of endurance than I could have hoped for at the beginning, So really

I was moved along unknowingly. Your patience, determination on a spiritual path are continually tested, you have to really want it. Then the gremlin thoughts pop in why bother, you never will get anywhere. Energy enhancement has been so useful in being able to see these negative thought patterns arising and nipping them in the bud when they crop up on a daily basis. You have to be continually on the alert for them.

I had learnt so much on the course to enhance my meditation practice and an extra bonus of being on the course was that I could develop my reiki practice.

Chapter 21

Reiki

I had always dreamed that I might be able to heal people but never thought that could be a realisation. Because I was interested in alternative ways of healing I was naturally drawn to reiki. I was pleased reiki was to be taught on the energy enhancement course as I was keen to develop my understanding of it. I had never read anything about it, never met anyone who had taught it before or experienced it, so I went with an open mind. I had no intention of asking inquisitive questions just for the sake of it, I just wanted to experience it for myself and come to my own conclusions. What follows is the testimonial that I wrote at the time.

On receiving my first Energy Enhancement Reiki initiation from Devi Dhyani in Spain 2003, I felt very peaceful. Blue and white energies kept expanding. As the session went on I started to cry, tears rolling down my cheeks and there was some jolting of my body but I was not unduly worried.

At the second session I felt I was being pulled up by one single hair on my head, up and up it pulled me. Later it felt as though a whole lot of stuff was coming out of my head into the universe. First my little finger felt numb then the other fingers followed suit. My feet also felt numb and slightly raised off the floor. My bottom also felt as though it was coming off the chair. Upwards and upwards was the movement. I felt emotionally tearful yet at the same time I felt very powerful, that I could move mountains with this strength.

On the third session I felt the heat of Devi's hands and a feeling of pushing me downwards. Initially again there was an image of white hands in the pray position and an opening up of my heart chakra, they felt more empowered this time. I felt snake like movements up and down my spine and I still felt numbness in my fingers tips but power going into them. I asked for help and the session ended with an image of wings flying slowly upwards, it was very beautiful and brought tears to my eyes, I wanted to fly too.

On the fourth session I felt similar sensations as before but this time the snake went outside my body, moving slowly upwards towards a star of light. My heart felt as though it was opening more and I felt a throbbing in my hands. A tornado started in my body, swirling very fast from the bottom of my spine upwards, eventually it slowed down to a snails pace, the energies had become gentler. From the white light I asked for help with my belly blockage, I used the white thread to weave in and out of this blockage and I sent it down into the fire in the centre of the earth.

When I received in my first initiations they was outside any previous experience I had ever had, they initiated me into beautiful spaces and feelings. They also allowed the clearing process to work. I cried at every session and it just felt as though I was getting rid of a lot of sadness, yet that sadness was mixed with the awesome beauty of the experience that also caused tears to well. The first initiation is about healing yourself and the second initiation is about healing others, which I had hesitantly done over the separating two years. Yet I lacked the confidence and the belief in myself that I had the necessary powers to heal. When I returned to Argentina, Devi repeated the first and second initiation before deciding if I was ready for Mastership. During the sessions I could feel my connection with the energies grow strong and I could act as a conduit for the energies to descend. The energies could be powerful and I was more open to their flow during the reiki sessions. Previously over the years I had felt the energies descend down into my body during meditation but not on the scale that reiki gave. The question arose what am I meant to do with them? Healing seemed a natural progression.

Devi is an intuitive gifted healer with supernatural psychic abilities. I consider myself blessed to have been taught by her, she is a true channeller of cosmic energies on this earth. I just simply sit on a chair in an upright position whilst she carries out the initiations on me. It is a very different way of learning, you experience reiki first then you learn more about it afterwards. I just made myself receptive and available. I did not feel the need to ask questions I just waited to see what the sessions would bring. Even after them I felt no need to query about them, the energies were just there and I accepted them as they were given.

When I returned to the course in Argentina I was not sure if I would be given the further reiki levels. At one point the energies from meditation were making me so light headed, it was agreed I would have a break from them to let them calm down before the next session. Most of the teaching was non verbal and Devi's hands did all the teaching that was necessary.

This happens very effectively with the Reiki teachings. By giving Reiki to a person they will know that the energies do exist and this will lead then to a greater understanding of what they and meditation is about. I have always wanted to help people through meditation and was pleased Reiki tied in with energy enhancement. I can feel the energies descend through me and be transmitted to the person being healed. It is that connection with a higher force and its flow, which created some very moving experiences I had with Devi. She is a wonderful teacher of it and her hands give all the learning necessary.

There has been an expansion of my energy fields that I would not have achieved on my own or elsewhere. To be able to use the energies in a healing way has exceeded my expectations. The techniques have deepened my spiritual understanding and also enhanced my spiritual practice. I intend to pass on this knowledge to those I meet on the meditation path.

The greatest joy for me has been able to use the energies for the benefit of others. Receiving reiki from my teacher was such a wonderful experience that I wished I could do the same for others. I returned from Argentina a Master in reiki and asked friends and relatives to come forward to receive treatments. There was a wide variety of emotional and physical problems, as well as those arising from personal coping abilities. I never told anyone about my personal experiences in reiki I just encouraged them to be open and give it a try. I was really gratified by the feedback I received, besides finding it very relaxing, most could experience the energies themselves or feel the heat generated by them. If someone I know is suffering from a difficulty or problem I just offer reiki and in every instance it has done good. Some effects are immediate i.e. shoulder or back pain relieved, others take a day or two such as lifting depression, increasing well being or ones own coping ability. Often long-standing problem situations have been relieved by the treatment. I do not make these claims myself it is just the feedback I receive. There might be an element of trying to please there but people who know me would understand I want honesty not praise. I have even given reiki to aid spiritual development as I feel it can be the first instance of feeling the energies and peace for most people. It is always an uplifting experience.

As I practice reiki I try to gain a deeper knowledge of how it can enhance my practice. I have used 'sounding' with it and was deeply interested to hear that Dr. Usui, Reiki's founder, originally came from a meditative background and used special sounding mantras. With the help of my meditation/sanskrit teacher in London I have been given beautiful sanskrit texts from the Atharva Veda and

Caraka Samhita Sutrasthana On the Fourfold Therapeutics to use. Also with his teaching of the correct pronunciation for the seed sounds of the chakras I have been developing these. I feel my knowledge is limited but I am always willing to expand it, reading books is not enough, it has to be experiential. Nothing rushed but just a slow observation of the effects when I use them.

The learning process just continues to expand, understanding about the energy pathways (nadis/meridians) I have since started to look into acupressure for myself, which led onto Acu yoga. This I have begun to incorporate in my teaching of yoga as it is a desire not to just teach yoga but how to use it in every life and for healing. I wish to teach life skills and as with acu yoga you can focus on special problem areas and help yourself.

What has been wonderful about my whole learning process is that everything ties into each other. I have not specifically set out to learn different subject or therapies they have revealed themselves to me. It is as though I was meant to learn about them and that a greater force has guided me. After having worked through my degree course for the Open University I did not want the hard slog of studying again. Exams, course work and dissertations took the joy from learning. I wanted to be spontaneously drawn to learn something, be it a book being given, an article catching my eye or something appearing on the Internet. Just that initial spark igniting the flame to learn, which connects you to an inward interest that you already possess. You do not realise it till it happens, it occurs naturally without effort.

The joy with reiki was with the laying on of hands, the knowledge was transmitted to me. I was fortunate to have had a preliminary knowledge of the energies, as I had practiced tai chi and qi gong for a number of years. I had a basic understanding of what they were and how they could be used.

Chapter 22

Tai Chi

It is easy to read about prana or chi in books but it is better to experience the energy first hand to gain a fuller understanding of what it is. Tai chi and qi gong is about accessing the universal energy that exists and getting it to flow through your body to move it. At the same time it can heal and increase well being.

It was in a qi gong class that I first felt this energy, it was a connection between my two hands whilst doing the standing postures. It felt the same as two separate facing magnets repelling. As I moved my hands together in a pulsing motion I could get a sense of an energy field expanding and contracting between them. As the energy increased through the lesson the space between grew larger and I could still feel the connecting energy, it often felt like holding a large squishy balloon. I thought this very fascinating at the time and just put it down to experience. I read books about the energy being stored in the Dan Tian of the physical body (in the navel area) and that you could also use it in a martial art form but my interest in qi gong waned and later was rekindled with the practice of tai chi.

Through yoga I had a basic understanding of the chakras, the energy centres in the spine but had never really concerned myself with them until on a weekend workshop where we did chakra balancing. I was amazed to feel the energy emanating from these points and this stirred my interest. Such experiences were something outside of my everyday experience so when they happened I just accepted them and put them to the back of my mind. It is only in retrospect that I realise they were my first taste of the energies that were to come.

My experience of energy was being gained piecemeal over the years. It started to be felt in my body but as my awareness of it increased I was able to detect people who had a high energy level. The first time this happened was when I was in the departure hall of Gatwick airport I was suddenly aware of a blast of energy, I looked to where I felt it come from and there at the far end of the hall was the monk, who would be teaching on the yoga holiday in Greece. I did not known it was him at the time, it was only when I was later introduced that I knew, yet I thought nothing more of it.

I felt naturally drawn to tai chi and when a class started in the village I was keen to join. I was enjoying being taught by our regular teacher, a young enthusiastic Scottish gentleman when one day he was ill and his tutor came to take the class. I was immediately taken by his quiet steady manner. He did not converse with the group just started into teaching and left without a word at the end. Instinct told me he could give the answers I needed and I asked my teacher to see if he would take me on a one to one basis. It was in the hope that the energies could be used to heal my skin complaint. He took me on. I appreciated the calm and stillness that surrounded his teaching, slowly when learning the tai chi form I began to get a better feel of the energies. When our regular teacher left he took over the class and I have been with him for over four years now but he is now moving on to practising falun gung, which he feels channels the energies more powerfully than tai chi.

In the tai chi classes all movement is tied in with using the energies to move the body not moving the body physically yourself. As the energies have increased in me over the years I feel them more powerfully, it is a joy to feel as though you are moving through an energy field with no effort at all. The arms can seem to float by themselves. After the class there is always a feeling of increased well-being and that the exercises had been beneficial.

It has been very useful doing standing meditations at the beginning of a tai chi class, which tied in with qi gong. It is something I would not have envisaged doing as I have always sat down to meditate. By moving and standing with the energies I tried to bring this understanding into my everyday life of housework and gardening. It was very different way of channelling the energies as opposed to what I had been doing in my yogic practice.

It is with meditation that I have felt the energies more dramatically and when I sit in meditation I never quite know what is in store for me. I always align my spine as I was taught; as there is a very fine central point that connects with the universal energies, aiding the meditative process. The energies dance, expand and contract; all manner of movement is felt but I just sit and observe. I do not get drawn in by them, I just let them run their course. I have become quite used to them now and try to learn what they are teaching me.

In meditation it is wise not to get distracted by such experiences, my understanding of them is that the energies cloak Consciousness and you need to go beyond them to get in touch with Reality. The energies are a communication channel to me, I notice them increasing with a particular piece of Sanskrit I am reading. This normally turns out to be a very relevant piece for me, which I can incorporate into my practice. The same when I am reading spiritual books the energies increase when something is important for me to take on board. It is always beneficial to listen to them and take note. Sometimes the energies are not so gentle, I often get daily surges of energy, which suddenly make me feel woozy but it happens so quickly that I recover before I realise just what has happened. It is all so much of a learning process for me and I just accept what is happening is because it is meant to be.

As I use the energies in reiki, tai chi, yoga and meditation, my confidence has grown on how to use them. On examining the word confidence I feel I need to explain the separate journey I have made to gain real confidence. Confidence that I never imagined having, which has enabled me to teach yoga and stand in front of a hall full of people and teach meditation.

Chapter 23

Confidence

I always admired, even envied those people who possessed confidence, they are not plagued by feelings self consciousness, inadequacy or embarrassment. If you could purchase confidence, it would be priceless. They say it can be taught, learnt in fact but I just think that is a cover up. Yes you can project it but underneath you still feel that well of inadequacy, which can seem fathomless. When you are faced with this abyss how can you drag out your own confidence, which is at its bottom?

Americans personify confidence; it is encouraged and valued in their education system and the whole American culture, so why is that not done in the English system? Why is true self-confidence possessed by so few of us? Dwelling on these larger issues does not aide the understanding of ones own lack of confidence in the beginning?

I was brought up in a caring family, but there were no expectations that I would achieve anything other than I would finish my schooling, get a job in an office/shop/factory, get married and raise a family. In some respects this is a blessing as no demands or stresses were put upon me. I was encouraged to be a caring and thoughtful daughter and that was valued more than anything else.

I was naturally quiet at school and generally well liked. I did not draw attention to myself and was well behaved. I understood the rules and knew what was expected of me. In Transactional Analysis terms I was 'a pleaser', and pleasing came easily to me. As a child I was aware that this worked for me and I carried on in my adult life. Operating in this way I gained my self esteem from those around me, if people liked me and thought well of me my confidence increased. But it was a very fragile thing and the slightest rude or nasty comment could shatter that illusion and I was faced with the void again. So I went through life in this way, I tended to avoid people who would take a dislike to me and hurl hurtful remarks at me. I filled my life with people who liked me and enjoyed my company whilst true self-confidence continued to elude me.

I performed many different outside roles in my life; model, counsellor, youth worker, voluntary worker. As I did the groundwork for these roles, I gained a confidence in my abilities but I was never able to project self-confidence in those abilities. There the difference lies, I could have a firm, quiet self belief that I had worked hard to achieve the status in the roles I played yet I could not broadcast this to those around me. I could not put myself forward and promote my abilities. Interviews filled me with dread, as I was unable to sing my own praises with enough verve to be convincing. I understood the need to act with confidence to gain other peoples respect and not be a push over, so I learnt to do act with confidence.

Having written that statement I am aware that I cannot sum up confidence in such a simplified manner. Since being on a spiritual journey my view of confidence has altered. I no longer view it in terms of just an 'individual's personal self-confidence' and now see it in a wider context. Confidence travels through many layers until it moves beyond the individual into the universal. It is natural to identify confidence with the small individualistic self but I discovered with meditation I could access the confidence of the universal Self. (I have chosen to used the word Self here as it is very relevant to the subject but the word Self can be substituted with earlier words I have used i.e. Consciousness, Reality, The Infinite and The Absolute – in short the unexplainable)

I had been meditating for several years before this came to light . At the end of the Creative Writing Course I had been on, we were required to give public readings of our favourite pieces of work. I had never spoken out in public nor used a microphone before but I was determined not to let the group down and just get on with it. I was hoping to get it over and done with early in the evening but unfortunately I was allocated a spot towards the end. Everything went well till my turn. The event was held in a room above a pub and just when it was my go a loud band downstairs started up, drowning out my voice. At that point I realised I could give up and sit down embarrassed or I could raise my voice and continue, I chose the latter. I received a round of applause at the end of my rendition and I felt a wave of achievement spread over me.

By turning inwards through meditation I am able to access the Self's natural confidence which in turn became my own confidence. Or to put it another way, now that I was in touch with the Self (Consciousness) there was no need of one's own self-confidence I was just able to act naturally without any self-awareness or criticism. It was freedom from all those nagging doubts in my head that continually found fault with my abilities. I never needed those gremlin thoughts and could well do without them. Having been on the Energy Enhancement course I was able to clearly identify all those negative thought forms that prevented me from fulfilling my potential. They were seen as blockages to my spiritual growth and which needed to be eliminated if I was to progress.

Meditation can encourage a witnessing of the thoughts that arise in the mind. If you try this out you will soon find a repetition of detrimental negative thoughts occurring in your mind. We allow ourselves to be open to this channel of abuse every minute of our lives, we think it is natural and normal to let our thoughts run wild. Free to come and go as they wish, as though we have no control over them. But we can have control; we can find the off button through meditation. You can ignore them, do not give them the energy of recognition and eventually they will lose their power and fade.

Meditation is all about finding the answer to 'Who am I?' Well you are certainly not your thoughts; they are the mind's creation from past experiences and events. Rarely can they have relevance to the present situation you find yourself in, far better to act in the Now with full awareness and allow your senses and brain react freshly to each situation as it presents itself. We do not have to tell the body to breathe each breath but it does it instinctively, so therefore we can trust our body and mind to react accordingly. With meditation you can reduce the mind chatter and acknowledge a natural response to each situation arising out of the space and silence of the universal Self.

Full awareness of this came to me when I had begun to teach meditation. For a long while I had been dismissing my teacher's advice that I should teach meditation. Up to that point I had been running on the small individual self's confidence, that I would never be good enough, that I had not accrued the set amount of knowledge. I could have written a long list of why I should not teach then suddenly out of the blue I wanted to teach. The confidence seemed to appear overnight; I was handing out posters, speaking to people to encourage them to learn meditation. The time was right to start and I started. I stood up and declared I was a meditation guide with assertion. That self belief came from the universal Self. Having said that the same Self, is the Self that exists within us, as without, there is no separation.

We are born with a belief in the Self but society and socialising techniques separate us from that true original Self, so that we become divided. We are cut off from our true heritage, where each person is valued in their own right. You are loved by the universal Self for who you are, not what you are. You do not have to achieve anything to be loved by the universal Self, you are loved because you are love. There is just love, waiting to be discovered. If you are loved, a natural confidence arises within you. It is not dependant on any person or situation; therefore it cannot be easily dismembered. One can hold one's head up because one is alive, we are born with a natural integrity that has never left us and is waiting to be found again.

That is what the journey of meditation is about, rediscovering your true Self, finding the answer to 'Who am I?' It is a journey inwards where the Self is waiting to be found, if you just look hard enough. Many great spiritual teachers of the past point you to the quest of 'Knowing Thyself.'

Unbeknown to me I was on that journey long before I acknowledged it to myself. We are all on that same journey whether we acknowledge it or not. Bit by bit when I was in contact with the Self, my true being, I had confidence in myself. By confidence I mean I was able to act naturally without negative thoughts pulling me down. I believed what I was doing was appropriate and not harmful to others. From this flowed a quiet sense of acceptance. There was no desire to win praise or draw attention to what I had done. It was reward enough to have done it. I admire people who clean toilets for a living or collect refuse, they can pride themselves in a job well done and have confidence they are doing a service to others. Too often we only attribute confidence to those who make the loudest noise and draw the most attention to their activities. But there exists a quiet confidence in every one of us that should be recognised and valued. It has an inner sense of rightfulness to it, nothing brash or loud.

When I have been in contact with my true being I have acted with the Self's confidence as described above. Outwardly, seen by others, as my own self-confidence but it does not belong to me personally, although I am able to benefit from it. Another word that can be used instead of the Self can be Being, it describes the same universal spirit or soul that encompasses everything. You cannot touch it and more often than not you cannot see it, it is just knowable. On rare occasions I have been able to see Being in a person's eyes and I can instantly recognise it. This became more observable with the birth of my young nephew.

Chapter 24

Being

I have had the great fortune recently to observe a young baby at close quarters. He was termed a miracle baby in that it took nine attempts at IVF to conceive him and on the final try when my brother and sister in law had given up hope it happened. I do not know if it was because he was so much wanted that inclined him to a delightful predisposition. He smiles and chuckles at anything and everyone. He spends most of his time in joyous contentment.

My guru had told me many times that a newborn baby is in bliss and that one could learn much by observing them and being in their presence. I paid lip service to this; I had brought up two children of my own and had cared for many others in my lifetime. Yes they were delightful, perfect, innocent, small human beings who have a charm all of their own but there were also the screams, dirty nappies, constant demands for food and attention. Caught up in the web of caring leaves little time to stand back and observe them objectively. They are loveable and mainly that is all that one sees. At the time when my children were very young, I did not understand what meditation was all about, let alone identify if they were indeed in a meditative state themselves.

Spending time with my nephew has aided my understanding of what the bliss of Being is in reality. At the time of writing he is six months old and sitting upright with support, his eyes take in everything he sees. He is fascinated by the way I eat and watches every movement I make. He constantly watches my reactions and is ever ready to catch my eye and make me smile. He really appreciates the attention I give him and he stares deeply into my eyes. There was one point when our eyes interlocked that I became aware that these were not just a young child's eyes looking at me but something more. Big blue eyes but they contained a beckoning to what was beyond them; I sensed they were a window to Being or at the very least his soul. It was like the shutters were open, the window was open, the curtains were open and it was there for me to see - the space of eternity. I stumbled to find the right words to encompass it, as in Tao terms it is the unspoken of, when it is spoken of, it loses its essence, it is not meant to be captured in mere words.

This was a puzzle I had pondered over many times since I started on my spiritual journey. The words Being and consciousness were brought to me but if you have never experienced them for yourself how to you know what they mean. You just have to take them on good authority that they do exist and hope that one day they will be revealed to you. I took it on board in the vedic tradition that we were all part of a whole, that there was no separation between us and Being, we were all part of the same thing. To try and get it clear in my mind I likened it to a big teapot full of tea. Being was the tea and it got poured out into different cups, in our planet be it animals, flowers, humans etc. When each died the tea got returned to the big teapot and then it was repoured into something different. Being was changeless in its various forms. Although this is an over simplified example it has helped me grapple with this unknown quantity. It was all part of the whole and nothing was separate.

Often God is separated from us and is perceived as something outside oneself to be worshipped. To be told you are God, God is you is a conundrum. It is the same as being told you are consciousness/Being and that you do not have to seek it, as you are it. I did question why I had not found it sooner if I had it all along. Why was it so elusive to find?

The mind-boggling even got larger when I was told that the world I lived in was not the real world but an illusory one called maya, that Being was in fact the reality. All I can say is that you sit tight and slowly all will be revealed. Just looking into the baby's eyes, I could start to begin to understand what was being said. I knew from my mediation experiences that I was not my mind or body, that I was something beyond. In those same states I could feel myself disappear, there was no person called me. I did not need to breathe or have bodily functions as there was no actual body. I cannot say I was ether, it was more of a nothingness. It was not an empty nothingness but a space containing all. In this realm the mind does not exist so there is no thinking, no brain to grapple to try and understand it. Just acceptance of what was. I now have a clearer picture that this would be Reality (another word for Being or consciousness) and that what I see in my life is the unreal. Saying unreal does not mean that it is not real but that it is a manifestation of the Real. Trees, houses, people even furniture are all manifestations of Being. There are multifarious forms of Reality filled with the same Being.

Just when I get an inkling of what is said, I am presented with the image of an empty house, each room is an empty space, so if that house was demolished, what happens to the empty space where does it go? It does not go anywhere because the space is still there. So it is with Being, it is always there. We are surrounded by it, it is outside and within, there is no separation between the two. The Being that I have within myself is the same Being as the person next to you has, it is one of the same we are made of the same stuff. Our problems arise because we do not recognise or acknowledge that this is the case. We highlight individuality which focuses on our differences, when we do this conflict arises and disagreements occur which lead to disharmony. We seem to thrive on this environment even though it leads to great unhappiness. We alienate each other although underneath this lies a yearning to become whole with another. We pair in partners to ward off the feeling of isolation and disconnection, yet all the time the thing that would satisfy us most is right under our noses, if only we chose to look – unity.

I return to looking, looking into my young nephew's eyes where a whole vista of understanding arose but that window of opportunity gets slowly obscured as a child develops. Not totally though, as you can catch a glimpse of it in any adult's eye. My greatest joy is seeing that flicker still alive in an adult's eye. It is a moment when you say 'yes' that's what it is all about. I really saw it, it was really there. Such moments cast away the doubts and Being shines through, which helps to propel oneself further on the spiritual path. As with anything a spiritual journey has its ups and downs and it is never easy.

Chapter 25

Acceptance

I had read in many different spiritual books that the keys to a spiritual life were surrender and acceptance. Okay I thought to myself I could run with this and it would be no problem, how wrong could I be.

After a long deliberation and finally concluding I was on my spiritual path, I had great difficulty incorporating it into my everyday life. My inner struggles were not visible to those close to me and even if I told them of my difficulties they had little understanding of what I was talking about. At times I wanted to scream and shout, as things got harder. I assume I wanted a pat on the back to say aren't you trying hard to be spiritual, how committed you are and how worthy. At that moment you see the games that are being played out by the ego, which wants to keep its own importance.

There is a fear that if the ego is diminished you will cease to exist at all. The ego has been constructed from many years of socialization, conditioning and education; we seem unable to think outside its constraints. We cannot comprehend that it can be an obstruction to our personal development, presenting a very limited and narrow outlook on life. A spiritual path challenges your beliefs, views, and constructs because if you wish to realise your potential you have to put them aside.

I was always amazed that out of the millions of people on this planet we each identify with our own life, we do not live collectively we live individually. Just as others, I viewed my own life as important and I constructed a field of existence around me where I felt safe to live in. As I went deeper into my spiritual practice, I realised this was holding me back and it was something I needed to let go of. The quandary was how could I let go of it all yet continue to live in the same environment. I yearned to escape and live in an isolated place by myself where I could follow my spiritual path unhindered. My spiritual guide made me realise this was not a feasible option. I had never been used to living on my own nor had isolated myself from my fellow human beings. I was a wife, mother, grandmother, friend, daughter; I questioned could I really turn my back on all those connections.

The best I could hope to get from living in isolation would be an increased spiritual depth or possibly enlightenment but what use would that be if I was on my own. Great for me but of no benefit to those close to me or to those I might meet in the future. Really it was just a pipe dream to hang onto, that everything in the garden would be wonderful if I did escape. Yet I did not have to escape to feel isolation; I often felt it when I was with people. I had a spiritual connection and would have been content to stay within its aura but I had to function as I would normally have done. To outsiders they would never have seen the hole in the stocking.

I was fully aware of it and assumed others would see it but it passed unnoticed. I was at a stage where I could feel at ease within a spiritual aura yet could not maintain it continually whilst I functioned in the everyday life. I flitted in and out of a meditative state becoming uneasy as my life tried to transform. Life felt like quick sand under my feet, there was no sure place to step. Anger and frustration at myself welled as I struggled to combine the separate forces in my life. I often doubted if it would be possible at all. All the time I had to continue to be 'normal' as I had done before, visit people as I had done before, do normal things like housework, gardening etc. I had thought it would all be so much easier and a smoother link combining spirituality into my life, not the internal disruption it was causing. I had paid lip service to it in the early days and, I had kept the two separate. The crunch had come with the reality of actually combining the two.

It was hard to practice acceptance with all the confusion and turmoil. I had imagined by proclaiming you were on a spiritual path that everything would become easier. In reality it became a lot harder. You expect people to understand what it is like but I kept most of my experiences and feelings to myself. I wanted understanding but how could I expect it when I found things very difficult to comprehend myself. My experiences were new to me and I had nothing to gauge them by. How much harder it would be for those who had little spiritual understanding. A friend reminded me to look back to how I was at the beginning and my miscomprehension about it all. Reminding me I had travelled along the spiritual path and those around me had not and I needed to show compassion and understanding.

As a balance to this I was always grateful to meet kindred souls who understood and were on a similar spiritual path themselves. I was not alone. I did not want separate lives, one spiritual, the other not. There was so much inner struggle and frustration with myself and others. Life seemed all too confusing to me, I tried my best but it was not working. I was trying to practice of accepting my life as it was but it was not working. It was because of this I decided to return to the Swamis in Spain to focus on my life and the relationships in it.

Chapter 26

Relationships

I returned to Spain in the summer of 2005 to repeat the whole of the Energy Enhancement course from level one to level four, to train as a teacher of level one and become a yoga teacher. What follows is the testimonial I wrote then. With the techniques of energy enhancement you deal with simpler straight forward negative energy blockages, the more difficult ones are left to the end and these were the ones I had to tackle.

I am now out in Spain training to be a yoga teacher with Energy Enhancement. I was previously out here with Satchi and Devi two years ago when I did the first part of the Energy Enhancement course. I later completed it in Argentina this year. I needed that gap in between to assimilate what I had learned and put it into practice. I teach meditation and have found it very helpful with my own personal growth as well as progressing on my spiritual path, so much so that I felt it would you very useful to those on a similar path and that I would like to teach it.

If you meditate long and hard enough you can resolve your life's problems but that can take a lifetime and I felt I could not wait that long, I wanted things to happen now. That's is why Satchi's and Devi's course appealed to me, it was all about doing, not just talking about it. It is experiential, you learn by doing, it is not some other person's experience, it is your own that you work on. Only by doing do you learn, you are given the necessary techniques to tackle negative thought forms in your life and you work through meditation to eliminate them. It saves hours of psychoanalysis; it is not necessary to rake up the past in fine detail. You can acknowledge past events and how they affected you. Recognising them intellectually is the first step but then you use the techniques taught to get rid of them.

I thought I would go through and share the processes that have occurred for me over the last few days. It is just a report of things as they are, no embellishments or make believe. Sometimes I am not too happy with the 'official' words to describe the processes but use them I will. Everyone attaches their own meaning to a word due to past experiences, so this has to be born in mind. A word is only a label and there is a need to go beyond that label.

Four days ago I was awoken early in the morning with a dream, one of those where you get caught up with anger, something was being taken away from me so I wanted to hide it. I was going to hide it in a florist shop and there was a door at the end with a woman and that was when I woke up. Dreams often have hidden messages for you, if only you listen and I tried to find out what it was.

In the dream the girl had felt anger towards her parents and that her sexuality had been restricted in the past. I tied this in with my own personal experiences at nineteen when a man tried to rape me. I had to fight like an animal to keep him off and it was a very nasty experience. Strangely enough another girl was raped at the same time nearby but she was murdered. I considered myself lucky and tried to get on with my life. So this was what I intended to use the techniques on. The attempted rape is labelled a blockage, meaning a negative energy form that is preventing my spiritual growth and that it needed to be destroyed in order to be free of it. Thus being able to develop along the spiritual path. I saw the attempted rape as an image of a thick tarry mass that would not shift despite all the techniques I was using to get rid of it. Then I asked myself what would shift tar? Heat. Where was the hottest place on earth? The centre of the earth. I took it there and it turned white, then I put it into a cauldron and it poured out.

On talking this process over with Satchi and Devi I realised that the attempted rape had caused me to distance myself from men inside, just in case they violated me again. I make the distinction of internal thinking and outward thinking. That was internal thinking, outwardly I enjoyed men's company and worked in all male environments, it was as though I was trying to regain my trust in men. Realising this in meditation made me tearful, because I wanted to be free of the internal negative thinking and enjoy male company. There is also the quandary for women in general, with the attraction of the sexes; there is always a sexual aspect to male and female relationships. I did not want to be sexually abused and I felt my husband was always there to protect me from this.

I had another meditation on this subject and got the white light again and it was a disc. A shape from behind it appeared a black one, just like its shadow, like the moon coming from behind the sun. I tried to get rid of it but nothing happened then I thought I must have succeeded in getting rid of the negative thought forms. Satchi soon put me right, the blockage was distracting me; in this way the blockage was avoiding me destroying it, I was not thinking straight and that is what a blockage can make you do.

Satchi felt this was more than just a blockage, it was an implant which are much harder to destroy, therefore Satchi and Devi were going to join me and meditate on the same subject. Destroying implants was a more complex technique but we persisted for an hour or more. Eventually it was released and I felt a feeling of sadness and loss. Satchi said this is often the case when implants have been destroyed. When I was meditating I felt a lot of gases in my stomach and throat, Devi had the same and even headaches and body pain. Whilst doing this same process I felt a lot of blockages around my heart, so I lumped then together and tackled then in one go. As they released I felt an expanding in my heart area. It felt like a firework going off, with lots of sparkly bits descending downwards.

At this point Devi questioned if my base chakra connection to the centre of the earth was clear of blockages, this I checked and Satchi advised doing the same for my crown chakra to the centre of the universe. Blockages were found at different points and cleared. Whilst clearing them I had a lot of exploding gases in my stomach area when I worked on both areas. I spent a lot of time on this as there were several blockages found. After such a day of consciously meditating and before I dropped of to sleep that night I was visited by some small black whizzy things, which I grounded before going off to sleep.

The next morning saw me finishing of the job I had started the day before. I worked on clearing the blockages around my heart, as I carried on I felt my heart expanding and glowing with a joyous feeling arising within. After these negative energies were grounded, whilst doing yoga afterwards, I was able to do the forward bend fully for the first time in my life, with my arms beside my shins. The second meditation was to finish clearing any blockages out of the antahkarana, the connection between the crown chakra and the centre of the universe.

Satchi referred back to my exploding stomach whilst meditating and said this indicated a strong connection with another person and I was to check the base chakra connection between my husband and myself. This I did and found a blockage there. Satchi said other indications of blockage connections with other people could be a bad back, a reduction in energy or headaches. If you heal them you heal your connection with them and so you are able to feel better yourself.

In the following day meditating I rechecked my connection between my base chakra and the centre of the earth. I then chose to focus on my idea of the sloth in me for example not wishing to get out of bed early to meditate. Satchi pointed out that this was an avoidance tactic used by the blockage to stop me working on it and I was to go back to the point when I felt that feeling and ground that point, this in turn I did. The instance should always be specific not general.

This same day Satchi and Devi joined me in my meditation, I knew we had tough work ahead, as were to start tackling my relationship connection. During the meditation Satchi felt physical pains moving around his body, heart, head and teeth. Devi was also feeling a lot inside and it connected with an inner child within herself. I was still getting plenty of stomach pains and gases in my throat. As we worked on it very hard it would not shift and Satchi identified it as an implant.

Blockages and implants are no fault of the actual person, they are just taken over by them causing misery to themselves and others. My husband had a blockage of possession towards me and it was making both our lives a misery. The only way out of the cycle of misery was to use the techniques taught. We all worked hard on this area, when it was freed I rechecked my connection with my husband to see if it was flowing properly, it was. What I learnt from this process is that those people around us also define us and that in order to be free oneself, one has to heal those around you. Life is a psychic laboratory and by working there you can enhance your spiritual development, not just for yourself but for others as well.

This brings me to the final day of tackling my relationship problem because this was such an important issue I had to recheck that it was thoroughly cleared. Yet again my stomach was still really churning away and Satchi felt this indicated that it was more than a blockage in my partner it was an implant, this we worked on together. Satchi also asked me to consider the benefits for me to have this implant/blockage in my husband, to ask why my ego wanted it to remain. A few ideas came up that I felt safe and cared for, which was a protection against men violating me. That desire for protection had ensnared me. A fear of change and of freedom could be present in me. There was also the guilt feeling around the attempted rape that I had done something to cause it. A blockage does not allow for rational thinking and internally I felt it was safer to suffer the situation as it was, in order to keep my husband's love. These were all areas I worked on in the meditations. I was tired of the fears binding me and stopping my personal growth, so I worked away with enthusiasm alert to any distractions from the job in hand.

When I was getting the better of the implant I felt the spaces in which I meditated expand. I got an explosion of energy down the right hand side of my body. The energy was bumping around in my base chakra; in fact my whole body was pulsating with the energies. It felt as though there was static electricity all along my arms making the hairs stand up on end. As the energies grew stronger I felt lighter, happier and freer. My heart opened out to send blasts of energy and love out which returned back to me. Finally cleared my relationship implants.

This was not just a quest for spiritual growth it was the quest for enlightenment. It is the spiritual path I am on, these techniques are just part of it. The ancient scriptures are followed and hatha yoga is practiced, it is all part and parcel of the same thing. Satchi said we are only given these things when we are able to deal with them and now was the time for me to deal them.

There are also positive images whilst meditating and one was of a large bird soaring in the sky, floating on the thermals, being taken by the wind. That is the analogy of my quest. I want to be free to follow my soul's path; I want to be that bird. Out of this I was given a message "Let the soul sing its song through my heart".

The one advantage of being a bird, is that you have a bird's eye view of things. You can fly high on the thermals and look down on the earth below.

Chapter 27

Humanity

In recent events a tidal wave has taken 150,000 lives, that vast number seems incomprehensivible to the human mind and causes one to question the existence of God. The Archbishop of Canterbury in his New Year's speech focused on the point that it was one death multiplied by 150,000 (1 x 150,000) – only then we can begin to understand its magnitude.

Each and every one of us is affected by death of loved ones, there is no escape. The grief and sadness of the loss touches our very core. It also reminds us of our own impermanent existence on this earth, hence death often becomes a taboo subject. Grief can be hidden and tears shed behind closed doors, yet we are able to relate to another person's loss, as it triggers memories of those that have been lost by ourselves. Each person lost in the tragedy would have caused grief to the whole of their surrounding family and friends, multiply that by 150,000 and how many people directly are affected by the same cause of death? – Millions.

Because of our vast communication network today we hear the news immediately and react to it, so that same tragedy touches the hearts of people all around the world – it becomes a global grief. Throughout this devastating loss, the human spirit is allowed to shine. Money is sent from every country, many from families that can least afford it but it is not just the giving that counts, it is the feeling that accompanies it. A feeling of knowing what the remaining families are suffering, together with a desire to ease their pains. That is what is so heart warming to come out of the tragedy – a unity of human spirit. In today's world we become alienated individuals, centred in our own family and friends that we rarely look at the wider picture. Religion is disappearing out of many people's lives leaving a void, leaving the question why we are put on this planet?

We see the disintegration of our communities and society whereby life's viewpoint becomes a need to self protect from those that live outside us. It takes a tragedy like this or the twin towers to make us share our fears, the individual fears are those shared by everyone. Instead of seeing differences in others it is time when we can acknowledge the similarities that we share with others. The desire to feed and protect our families is universal and this is just one example of the commonality of human life. There comes a point where every person needs to recognise the unity of our existence. We are not just an isolated individual but part of a whole. The unity encompasses each and every person on this planet, it emanates from each individual's heart.

Seeing people out on the streets shaking buckets for the relief fund, shows people care enough to do something about it. Every person has that same ability but it takes a tragedy to give an opportunity for that kindness to be demonstrated. That kindness is universal, there are many such gifts that we are born with and all share. We need to stop and pause to acknowledge what we all share, instead of focusing on the differences. The world becomes a smaller place each day as our communication networks widen, now is the time to see our world as part of the whole not just separate countries with different interests. There are millions of people on this planet and we are all human beings, sharing the same feelings and emotions despite different circumstances and languages. Each of us has the gift of life, which we should be grateful for and from which we can learn. To learn that we are part of the whole, the key word is unity, look for what unites us not separates. Look at the wider picture, look to the skies at night, listen to a bird singing or listen to the silence.

There was a two-minute silence before the New Year in order to remember those that died, just as we do on Remembrance Sunday. Silence gives us a chance to pause and reflect but it can also give us an opportunity to experience being part of a whole. In those two minutes we are united as one, which in turn connects us to the universal. To feel part of the wider picture and rejoice.

Chapter 28

Unity

How to conclude a book about my spiritual path, when this is only the beginning, life presents an ongoing learning experience. I doubt on my deathbed I will feel that I have learned enough about living and all that life holds. I have been given a wonderful opportunity to learn, as we all have.

Admittedly my life at first glance might seem more easier than most but I can look back to my childhood after the Second World War when money was tight. At five when we were given a new council house, it seemed like a palace. Every new purchase to furnish it, be it a settee or a carpet was earned by my Dad's hard labour and we had to wait till he had earned it before buying. I can never forget the joy of choosing how to use his cigarette coupons to obtain some new casserole dishes for my mother. It taught me not to take things for granted, to appreciate what one had, not to expect, to enjoy what was freely given, like friendship and family – to enjoy the company of others. What gifts are bestowed on us every day, a smile from a stranger or a chat with someone in a queue. We are not alone we are part of a whole.

On my travelling around the world I am often struck by the similarity of everywhere and I don't just mean every city has a McDonald's. So often one cosmopolitan city can seem like any other that you have to recheck in your mind where you are. This happened at the time of writing when I was out in Argentina we travelled over to the Brazilian side to view the Iguazu waterfalls which was nearby. Whilst there our taxi driver arranged an evening entertainment for us, a dinner with local folklore singers and dancers. The food was 80 dishes from around the world and the diners numbered 1200. There we were all sitting in Brazil and the compere asked where people came from, the answers came Israel, Japan, Korea, Sweden, Czech Republic and the list went on. I was struck that we all were tourists having come to visit the falls, our aim was the same. We were united in that one aim.

Too often countries highlight their differences to create wars but today with telecommunications and the Internet available to everyone the world becomes a smaller place by the minute. I watched the Kumbamela, a religious festival in India which millions of people attend, and was surprised to see the use of computers to find lost children. It seemed 3,000 had been lost at the last one. Today's young people take all this technology for granted and do not wonder at its existence and its capabilities, as my generation tend to do.

Although mobile phones and computers increase the communication between people I often wonder at the quality of it. Banality often exists and replaces face-to-face contact between family and friends. Recognition as to the value of human interaction needs to happen. All round the world we are the same people in similar family structures and homes. Allowing for all the cultural variations we still have the need to love and be loved.

We breathe the same air, share the same space, we drink the same water, we look up to the same sun and moon. We are all part of the whole not just separate individuals trying to survive the best way we can in an alien world. We can look up at the night sky and see the stars and galaxies shining their light to us from afar and we wonder what is out there. But it is much harder for us to turn inwards and look for that same light within our being.

That same light can provide strength and comfort in the difficult times, healing and understanding in the good times. It is a light that burns constantly within each one of us, the light of consciousness. The inner light connects to the universal light and it is the same light. My hope by you reading to the end of my book is that you will acknowledge that light within for yourself.

Chapter 29

Know thyself

Before starting my spiritual journey I would have claimed to know myself but that was a surface knowing. When I started to look deeper at my life I found I did not know. I had played many different roles in my family, working and social life. I could even just act them out if I was not sure what to do. On reflection I was many different people, depending which situation you found me in. I have pondered and questioned, 'which one was the real me?' in all of this. I could see a similarity in the roles and thought there must be an underlying essence of me to be found. I had studied psychology and sociology and could reason things out on a mental level to understand why I behaved in certain ways but I was left with an empty feeling inside that did not tell me who I really was.

So often in my life I had left out consideration for myself. I hoped my needs would be met and in a way I set out to get them met. I never expected things to be handed to me on a plate. I knew if I wanted anything I had to work hard for it. In my early twenties that meant taking evening and weekend bar work on top of my ordinary job, to be able to afford travelling and holidaying abroad. I understood marriage was all about compromise if it was to succeed. But sometimes life just seemed hard work. I did not seem to have the capability to let life wash over me and 'go with the flow'. I would have liked to have these traits but they were not in my character, I had responsibilities and commitments.

When they diminished I found myself in my early fifties still not knowing who I was. Who was this person who was called Vanessa. Those knowing me might have thought they knew me but I did not know myself. When I read in a spiritual book the way to enlightenment was by 'knowing yourself', I wondered how that could be done.

We are born onto this earth to develop spiritually that is why we have been given a physical body and all its senses. We are here to enjoy life, to find the joy in living, we were not put here to be weighed down with stresses and worry. I have been very fortunate to have found my spiritual path. I now know it was there all the time I just did not see it.

Over the last few years I have been peeling away the onion layers of my life and through meditative awareness have been able to look at it in more detail. In this book I have highlighted certain turning points, which I hope you the reader will have been able to identify with. Perhaps they are not similar to your own but they might have the ability to trigger remembrance of other situations. Although this book is a personal account, it is just a story of one person's life, my life story. Each one of us has their particular story to tell, each one is valid as the next.

I have been very fortunate to have found meditation, it was not what I thought it was about originally. Just sitting still in silence and accessing the peace within. The mental mind chatter is overwhelming at first and needs to be quietened and the best way to do that is clear out the clutter from the mind. To review negative past events and situations, to let them go. They happened in the past, it is the now that matters. In reality the past is just electrical currents stored in the brain. Too much of our time is spent reliving the past at the expense of the now, the present moment gets overlooked. Joy is found in the present moment, being alive to what presents itself in the moment. If the mind is clear and free from expectations the present moment can hold so much.

In our present day living we allow our mind to take control. We listen to its incessant chatter and we believe it is true. Too much of our time is spent in a mental world of activity, which creates stress, anxiety and fatigue. Today with our advanced telecommunication networks, television, computers, phones and computer games rule most young lives. There is no balance to this continual mind activity. Often silence can be seen as threatening and a void to be quickly filled with more activity. Silence gets misunderstood, its healing ability being lost, its nurturing remaining unfelt. It is the balm to sooth all ills if only it were listened to.

It has been through meditation and silence, I have come to review my life. I have found it easier to say who I am not, than say with confidence who I am. I have spent time eliminating negative thought patterns and behaviour, in fact I am still working on many as I write but what I have discovered by doing this I am none of these. The more I work with spiritual energies the more I am connected to them. The more I am in touch with them the more I can see they are the real me. I feel the connection to Consciousness, I can feel its energies course through my body. They bring serenity and peace. Initially I felt this while meditating but now that has spilled over into my everyday life. Not all of the time just some of it.

Through meditation I have been able to dissolve the separation that existed between my spiritual and everyday life. I have learnt that everything is spiritual and I have been brought to this understanding because of my progression along my spiritual path. It has been an unravelling of what it truly means. I have been untangled the ball of wool which was my life. This book bears witness to the strings I have pulled out of it. The realisation is that I was a spiritual being all along, I consist of a body, mind and spirit, I just lost sight of it.

When I look inward I see Consciousness / Reality / Being / the Absolute or whichever name you choose to give it. That

Consciousness connects each and everyone of us, we are all part of the whole. Each one of us is Consciousness, that is who we really are. Yes we do still have our life story of who we are, what we do etc. But do not believe that you are just that life story, you are so much more than that. You are the essence that gives life to everything. It is very freeing to come to this realisation. You can play the game of life with greater detachment and appreciate it for what it is – your life's story.

I have outlined my life's story in this book, it has been a journey to this realisation. By being the observer of your own life you tend to get occurrences and events more in perspective, I do not now get so easily pulled this way and that by events or people. As I have tried to empty my mind, I have had to let go of irritation and grudges I might hold because they interfere with the peace. As you get rid of this rubbish it gives a space for beauty to flow in and I know which one I prefer. My word of advice would be 'be kind to yourself, be your own best mate, care for yourself, be compassionate and thoughtful to yourself'. Your self is a reflection of the big Self.

I can more easily connect to Consciousness (big Self) and see things from a different perspective, from the big 'I' instead of from the little 'i' stance (individual self). Concentrate on your own life not other peoples. I have learnt to let people live their own lives, including those close, they do not need my approval on what they do. Try acceptance for how people are, do not judge or give opinions on what is right or wrong for them. But most of all accept your self, that you are good enough as you are, give up guilt and regret. Forgive the past and live in the now, drop the weight of the past.

Meditation is all about de-cluttering the mind as only by throwing out the clutter can you make room for the spirit to flow in. Letting go is not easy but I hope that you can see from what I have written it is possible. We do not need a storehouse of negative thinking to disrupt our lives and stop us living life to our full potential.

Letting go of life's excess baggage is great, when that weight is lifted there is a lightening of the soul, it is free to enjoy life's simple pleasures. When you are in touch with your spiritual side you feel whole not fragmented, you feel connected and supported. Fears are eliminated and you see them for what they are, created thoughts. Fears keeps us small and stop us from what we really want to do, see them for what they are.

I have shown the path I have travelled, the boulders I have walked round, the stones in my shoes and I would not have changed a thing. I have learnt more from bad situations than I ever could from good ones. It is only difficult events that encourage a turning inwards to deal with them. The more you do, the easier it gets. I 'know myself' better from having trod the path.

But here the difference comes with, 'know thyself". Know yourself to be connected to something greater, to be part of the whole, to discover the universal spirit that encompasses everything. I have learnt so much and grown spiritually on my journey. The revelation is that I was on my spiritual path all along but I just did not know it. My wish for you the reader is that you too will listen to the call of your heart and acknowledge the spirit within.

Vanessa regularly teaches meditation and meditative yoga (which encompasses deep relaxation and meditation) from her home in West Sussex. She also holds classes in Brighton and London.

Vanessa has been practicing yoga for over twenty-two years and it was yoga that led her to meditation. She was introduced to her Advaita meditation teacher ten years ago. He is a Sanskrit Scholar of 35 years standing and also teaches her the ancient language of Sanskrit, which allows her to read and sound the ancient vedic teachings directly.

Vanessa learnt Energy Enhancement Meditation techniques in Spain and Argentina and in 2005 trained to teach it. She teaches the first eight initiations for those wishing to deepen their meditation practice.

As a Reiki Master she offers treatments and attunements. She has been practicing tai chi and qi gong for over six years. She encompasses her counselling and person centred art to help those on a spiritual path on a one to one basis. She finds all these areas entwine together which enable her to give a balanced and well-grounded experience. Her learning is on going and she regularly attends workshops, lectures and retreats in order to deepen her understanding.